A Time to Be Born—
A Time to Die

A Time to Be Born—

A Time to Die

ROBERT L. SHORT

HARPER & ROW, PUBLISHERS

New York, Evanston, San Francisco, London

FIRST EDITION

Designed by Patricia Dunbar

Library of Congress Cataloging in Publication Data

Short, Robert L
 A time to be born—a time to die.
 Includes bibliographical references.
 1. Bible. O.T. Ecclesiastes—Criticism, interpretation, etc. I. Title.
BS1475.2.S56 1973 223'.8'066 72–78058
ISBN 0–06–067676–0
ISBN 0–06–067677–9 (pbk.)

To my sweet little daughter, Rebecca Grace—

whose given names, chosen as they were from the Old and New Testaments respectively, will I hope always be at least a reminder to her that neither Testament can ever really be appreciated, understood or enjoyed without the other.

I would earnestly beg and warn every devout Christian not to be offended at the homely speech and story which so often meet him in the Old Testament, and not to doubt, however poor it appears, that here are words, works, judgments and deeds of supreme divine majesty and wisdom. . . . Here thou shalt find the swaddling clothes and crib in which Christ lies, and to which the angel directs the shepherds. Poor and tiny clothes they are; but precious is the treasure, Christ, who nestles in them.

—Martin Luther

Acknowledgment is gratefully extended to the following for permission to photograph material:

2:2 From the motion picture "The Graduate." A Mike Nichols-Lawrence Turman Production, a Joseph E. Levine Presentation. Copyright © 1967 by Avco Embassy Pictures Corp.

2:10 Reproduced by special permission of *Playboy Magazine*; copyright © 1972 by Playboy. PLAYBOY, PLAYMATE and the RABBIT HEAD Design are marks of PLAYBOY, Reg. U.S. Pat. Off.

3:5 *Embrace*, by Sculptor, Gleb Derujinsky.

3:6 *Chicago Today* photo.

3:7 Poster by Studio One (T/A Poster Prints) from artwork by Michael V. Lynne, copyright 1969.

3:9 Painting by Helmut K. Wimmer, Hayden Planetarium, New York.

3:19 Gallery view showing detail of *Guernica* by Pablo Picasso (1937, May-early June). Oil on canvas, 11′5½″ x 25′5¾″. On extended loan from the artist to The Museum of Modern Art, New York.

4:3 Copyright 1971, Talon Division of Textron.

4:7 Copyright Brilliant Enterprises, San Francisco, 1971.

4:16 Drawing by David Levine. Reprinted with permission from *The New York Review of Books*. Copyright © 1968 The New York Review.

5:1 Poster text and design © Abbey Press. St. Meinrad, Indiana. Reprinted with permission.

5:18 Copyright Brilliant Enterprises, San Francisco, 1968.

5:20 Copyright Brilliant Enterprises, San Francisco, 1972.

6:2 Poster by Grey-North Advertising, Inc.

6:12 Copyright Brilliant Enterprises, San Francisco, 1971.

7:17 WSPD TV Channel 13, Toledo, Ohio.

7:23 Copyright Brilliant Enterprises, San Francisco, 1969.

7:24 © 1972 by The New York Times Company. Reprinted by permission.

7:27 Copyright Brilliant Enterprises, San Francisco, 1967.

7:28 Gallery view showing detail of *Seated Bather* by Pablo Picasso (early 1930). Oil on canvas, 64½″ x 51″. Collection, The Museum of Modern Art, New York. Mrs. Simon Guggenheim Fund.

8:15 Service Marks of American Dairy Queen Corporation.

8:17 Copyright Brilliant Enterprises, San Francisco, 1970.

9:11 Reprinted with the permission of Buzza/Gibson.

9:14 Painting *The Philosopher's Conquest* by G. De Chirico: Courtesy of The Art Institute of Chicago.

10:3 Poster by Robert H. Moore.

10:14 © 1972 by The New York Times Company. Reprinted by permission.

11:1 7UP and UN are trademarks of the Seven Up Company.

12:1 Gallery view showing painting by Ivan Albright: Courtesy of The Art Institute of Chicago.

Grateful acknowledgment is also given to Pete Seeger for "Turn! Turn! Turn! To Everything There Is a Season." TRO © 1968 Melody Trails, New York

Acknowledgments

"There is no end to all the books that are made, and much study will wear one's strength away" (Eccles. 12:12). Long ago I learned that my friend and teacher Ecclesiastes always speaks the truth, and certainly this verse is no exception. Indeed my own strength would have been well worn away long before *this* book was made had I not been the fortunate recipient of much first-rate help from many generous and kind sources. Although I accept full responsibility for the views expressed herein, there are two young and very fine Old Testament scholars who deserve special thanks for helping me to formulate such views as they are. Professors Wolfgang Roth and James Weimer of Garrett and Mc-Cormick Theological Seminaries respectively, are men with such love for teaching and for the Old Testament that they cannot be dismayed even by students the likes of me, who must be "grafted in" from another area of specialization. I am also greatly indebted to my major professor, Dr. Philip S. Watson of Garrett, truly a wise man in the tradition of Eccles. 8:1. Knowing full well I was supposed to be laboring among the pages of systematic theology, he nevertheless bore with patient good humor my "unsystematic" preoccupation with the Old Testament. Dr. Paul Hessert has been very helpful to me in the area of "Media Theology," which is also the title of an excellent course that he and Professor D. J. Furnish have taught at Garrett. Professors Egon Gerdes of Garrett, Paul Blanton and Edmund Perry of Northwestern University, are also very talented teachers to whom I owe sincere thanks.

While gathering pictures for this book I became more and more struck by similarities in the thinking of Ecclesiastes, the Bible's "modern man," and a modern man of our own time, Mr.

Ashleigh Brilliant, creator of the very fresh and popular "Pot-Shot" postcards. The fact that Mr. Brilliant can hold such an accurate mirror up to our own time and also—without even trying—to the thought of Ecclesiastes, speaks not only of the truth in Mr. Brilliant's work but also of the modernity of Ecclesiastes.

The men with whom I have enjoyed the closest friendship over the years are also, strangely enough, men who enjoy a good theological tussle as much as I—Augusto Larreta, John W. Mills and Charles Schulz. This has led me to conclude that no-holds-barred theological discussion is just that pinch of spice absolutely necessary to all true and lasting friendships. Also, I do not want to miss another opportunity to say "Thank you" to the Reverends Clayton Feaver and Finis Crutchfield, two very fine Oklahomans who happened to be on hand to lend friendly and expert assistance at the whelping of a certain theological puppy; and also to Professor John Deschner, of the Perkins School of Theology, whose inspiration generated so much sheer excitement in me that I managed to graduate from that singular institution in spite of my own best efforts to the contrary.

In Evanston, the families of Geoffrey Gilbert and Mrs. James Timothy have been much more than good neighbors. Howard Leibman and Roosevelt Robinson have somehow kept me in photographic equipment through the strange vicissitudes of time and chance. The friendship and help of Joe Weichselbaum, a survivor of the infamous Auschwitz concentration camp, is also greatly appreciated.

The efficient ladies and gentlemen at Astra Photo Service in Chicago, who have done all of my darkroom work for many years now, are certainly to be commended for their excellent work. (For those who might be interested, all pictures in this book were shot with Nikon equipment, available light and Tri-X film at 400 ASA.) At Harper & Row I am lucky to have such a friend and editor as Marie Cantlon. I am also indebted to the many audiences who over the years have seen the nucleus of this book in the form of a color-slide presentation. Their perceptive comments and questions have sharpened my own appreciation for the truly incredible power and richness concentrated in the Book of Ecclesiastes.

As for my wife, there is little I can say that would do justice to her constant help and support. She has, however, enabled me fully to experience the wisdom behind Ecclesiastes' words: "Enjoy life with a woman you love, all the days of your life that God gives you under the sun . . ." (Eccles. 9:9).

Ecclesiastes—"The Truest Of All Books"

That mortal man who hath more of joy than sorrow in him, that mortal man cannot be true—not true, or undeveloped. With books the same. The truest of all men was the Man of Sorrows, and the truest of all books is . . . Ecclesiastes . . . the fine hammered steel of woe.

—Melville, *Moby Dick,* Chap. xcvii

So far as I can see from . . . observing you, yours is the way of life, the way of thought, of feeling, and of acting, of the Preacher of Ecclesiastes. I know of no better way. For of all that I have ever seen or learned, that book seems to me the noblest, the wisest, and the most powerful expression of man's life upon this earth—and also the highest flower of poetry, eloquence, and truth. I am not given to dogmatic judgments in the matter of literary creation, but if I had to make one I could only say that Ecclesiastes is the greatest single piece of writing I have ever known, and the wisdom expressed in it the most lasting and profound.

—Thomas Wolfe, *You Can't Go Home Again,*
Chap. 47

I

Ecclesiastes and the Photograph: Truest to Life

Who wants to see life as it is, if they can help it? It's the three Gorgons in one. You look into their faces and turn to stone. Or it's Pan. You see him and you die—that is, inside you—and have to go on living as a ghost.

—Eugene O'Neill, *Long Day's Journey into Night*[1]

To love ugliness—yes, quite right! For if I am (as indeed I am) flesh and blood, a being of senses, an animal creation, then spirit is the most terrible thing for me, terrible as death, and to love spirit is the most terrible thing of all. So too Christianity understands it, it teaches that to love God means to die, to die to the world, the worst of all torments. . . . That is why, in times when Christianity was taken seriously, those who took it seriously made use of a death's head for their constant contemplation. . . . a death's head was the most significant symbol.

—Kierkegaard, *The Last Years*[2]

The wise man is the one who sees reality as it is, and who sees into the depths of things. That is why only that man is wise who sees reality in God. To understand reality is not the same as to know about outward events. It is to perceive the essential nature of things. The best-informed man is not necessarily the wisest. Indeed there is a danger that precisely in the multiplicity of his knowledge he will lose sight of what is essential. But on the other hand knowledge of an apparently trivial detail quite often makes it possible to see into the depths of things. And so the wise man will seek to acquire the best possible knowledge about events, but always without becoming dependent on this knowledge. To recognize the significant in the factual is wisdom.

—Bonhoeffer, *Ethics*[3]

Ecclesiastes tried to find pleasing ways to express the honest truth.

—Ecclesiastes 12:10

The author of the Book of Job was a consummate dramatist. The psalmist was a lyrical poet. The author of Jonah knew how to tell a fascinating short story, and the authors of Genesis and Exodus were "historical novelists" who could recount powerful sagas of epic proportions. Ecclesiastes, or "the Preacher," was also no mean poet, but fundamentally he was an artist of another sort: He was a photographer. His method of searching for life's meaning was, as he tells us, to give himself "over to observing and investigating, with the use of wisdom, everything that is done under the sun. . . . I have seen all the works that are done under the sun, and behold, all is vanity and chasing the wind" (1:13-14).

"Under the sun"! This phrase, constantly repeated by Ecclesiastes, is significant for him in three ways. First, as the sun was Ecclesiastes' timepiece or "clock," it was a fitting symbol for the way in which he saw all things *under the control* of the inexorable hand of fate. "For all things are governed by time and chance" (9:11). Men can no more be the master of their own fates than they can control the movement of the sun or the sweeping hands of time. Indeed, Ecclesiastes may well have furnished the inspiration for Melville's famous statement:

Is it I, God, or who, that lifts this arm? But if the great sun move not of himself; but is an errand-boy in heaven; nor one single star can revolve, but by some invisible power; how then can this one small heart beat; this one small brain think thoughts; unless God does that beating, does that thinking, does that living, and not I. By heaven, man, we are turned round and round in this world, like yonder windlass, and Fate is the handspike.[4]

The fact that we men "are turned round and round in this world, like yonder windlass," points to Ecclesiastes' second reason for seeing the sun as such a significant symbol. Because he believes that the purpose behind men's lives—if any—is hidden from them, all existence then takes on the meaninglessness of never-ending cycles—cycles which continually turn round and round but never really get anywhere. As far as Ecclesiastes' eyes can tell him, the entire universe is "spinning its wheels." That this basically hopeless turning includes *all* things is shown by the apparent fact that it not only includes the sun itself, but also "everything under the sun," as represented by the wind, the waters and the "generations" (1:4-7).

But it is the third aspect of Ecclesiastes' fascination for the sun that we are more concerned with here: it was the sun that made possible Ecclesiastes' "all-important activity of observation." Without sunlight, Ecclesiastes' method of getting to the bottom of things by "observing . . . everything that is done under the sun," would have been as frustrated as the earliest method of photography, also completely dependent on the sun's strong light to "observe" its images.

The word "photograph" means "written with light." In this sense no other biblical author was as much a "photographer" as Ecclesiastes, his book being written almost entirely on the basis of what he could actually *see* "under the sun." This is why his book, more than any other book of the Bible, lends itself so easily to photographic interpretation. What he tells us that he saw and drew his conclusions from, was simply life itself; and for this reason what he saw was really not so different from what men *still* see every day of their lives. But of course there is a world of difference between sight and insight, between those who *really* see and, as Jesus could say,

3

those who "indeed see but never perceive" (Mt. 13:14). And Ecclesiastes knew how to see *and* to perceive. That is, he also knew how to see *through* the concrete particulars of the world to conclusions of a deeper and more universal significance.

This is why Ecclesiastes can be especially helpful to us today. In many important ways his time and our time are uniquely alike. It is almost as if time itself has come full circle so that men are once more living in the time of Ecclesiastes. Therefore when we couple his commentary on "everything under the sun" with corresponding images from the gamut of life today, the result can be not only a greater appreciation of *his* many insights, but also the appropriation of these insights as *our own* when we see their special applicability in interpreting and meeting the challenges of our time.

What kind of photographer was Ecclesiastes? This may come as a shock to a certain French gentleman, but Ecclesiastes was the Henri Cartier-Bresson of the Old Testament! This man, whom many regard as the greatest living photographer, would have been at least a great favorite of Ecclesiastes. For the pictures of Cartier-Bresson, like those of Ecclesiastes, are known for their blunt honesty about life and the fact that they "tell it like it is." Cartier-Bresson is one of the few photographers who fully exploit the genius of the camera, which is to "never lie." His pictures, always shot with only whatever light is available, are never in any way "artificial" or contrived. They are never posed or arranged or altered by darkroom technique—they are not even cropped! "One has no right to use tricks or to play around with reality. . . . The thing to be feared most," he says, "is the contrary to life."[5] His purpose, Cartier-Bresson tells us in words that would have delighted Ecclesiastes' heart, is "to come to grips with life itself."[6] He therefore shuns the anecdotal and the "cute," the picturesque and the "pretty."

Ecclesiastes, like Cartier-Bresson, would also have been strictly a black-and-white photographer. In another statement sounding remarkably like our Preacher, Cartier-Bresson tells us, "My photographs are variations on the same theme: Man and his destiny."[7] Ecclesiastes, likewise preoccupied with the more *basic* struggles of men's lives—good vs. evil, wisdom vs. foolishness, light vs. darkness—would also have agreed with Cartier-Bresson that "color doesn't add anything, it detracts."[8]

And it is certainly true that Ecclesiastes, again like Cartier-Bresson, would have been only a "still" photographer. As Cartier-Bresson points out, in a movie it is primarily the *story* we are interested in. But still photography, he says, "is a strictly visual medium, grasping at the evidence of reality."[9] This is why many commentators, insisting on "a foolish consistency . . . the hobgoblin of little minds," as Emerson put it, have complained that Ecclesiastes is too "fragmentary" and "disjointed," with little or no discernible plan or logical development. But how often does *life itself* exhibit this kind of smoothly flowing continuity? Has it not been more aptly described as "a heap of broken images" or as "one damned thing after another"? It is precisely because Ecclesiastes is so true to life that reading his book is very much like looking at a long series of still photographs, all of them slices of life of one-hundredth second, but each possessing its own special integrity and therefore each demanding the viewer's *own* rapt "stillness."

"To me," says Cartier-Bresson, "the camera is a prolongation of my eye. The instantaneous combination of eye, heart, and head seems essential to me."[10] What better one-line summation could be found for the Preacher's brief but astonishingly pregnant book than "the instantaneous combination of eye, heart, and head"? For these are the same essentials Ecclesiastes is commending to us in *his* concluding summation: "Let your heart and your eyes show you the way. But also be sure of this: God will judge whether you have made good use of all he has given you" (11:9). Even Cartier-Bresson's *method* of picture taking and the reason he gives for it sound strangely similar to what von Rad calls "that utter insecurity in regard to life which Ecclesiastes is never weary of revealing from every angle."[11] The *modern* photographer puts it this way: "Within [the discipline of respect for reality] there are infinite variations. I weave around the subject like the referee in a boxing match. We [photographers] are passive onlookers in a world that moves perpetually."[12] Also, what has been said of Cartier-Bresson's pictures can just as aptly describe the "pictures" of Ecclesiastes: "These photographs ask questions: the riddle is part of their strength."[13]

I have chosen to illustrate many of Ecclesiastes' words with pictures which themselves involve words. But again this is entirely in keeping with Ecclesiastes' own way of observing. For apparently much of his time was spent "testing and amending and fashioning many proverbs with great care" (12:9). Indeed his book contains numerous proverbs that were current in his time, but he always expresses them with the personal twist of his own "amending." If Ecclesiastes were living today, he would again be forced to deal with popular bits of wisdom since we once more live in an age of the "proverb." We wear our hearts on our automobile bumpers, and the words of the prophets are written on the subway walls and tenement halls. This plenitude of capsule wisdom is just one more way in which Ecclesiastes' time was so amazingly like our own.

Along with the following new translation, the photographs are also mine. (Even the picture from *The Graduate* was simply taken from the screen as I watched that remarkable film for the umpteenth time.) Using only my own pictures was not done because of any "vanity" on my part, I hope, but simply in order to prove a point: that what Ecclesiastes saw and drew his conclusions from was certainly no more than what can be seen by any "one man in his time."

1: 1 The words of Ecclesiastes, David's son, King in Jerusalem:

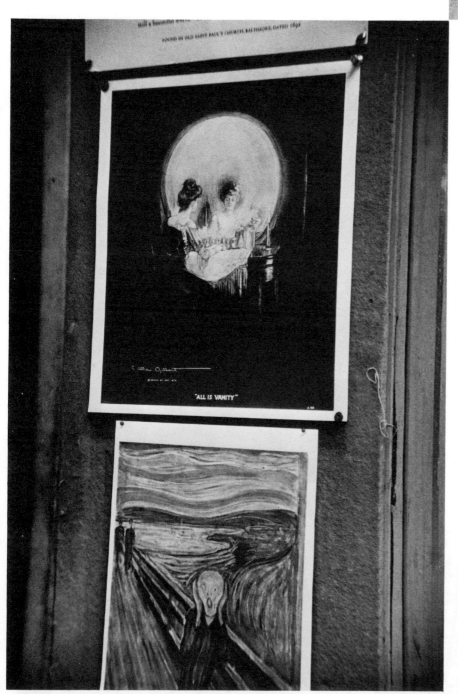

2 Futile, empty and meaningless! says Ecclesiastes. Fleeting, incomprehensible and pointless! All things are vanity![14]

3 What is there of real permanence that a man gains by all his trouble and effort during his brief lifetime under the sun?

4 One generation goes, another generation comes, but the earth remains essentially the same.

5 The sun also rises only to disappear over the horizon; then round it goes to rise and set again.

6 The wind blows south, then blows north; round and round it blows, returning full circle.

7 All the rivers flow into the sea, and yet the sea is never full, even though the rivers still are flowing.

8 Words cannot describe the weariness of all things.

The eye is not satisfied with its seeing, nor the ear
filled with its hearing.

9 Just as nature will continue to be what it has
been, human nature will likewise continue
to be what it has been.

There is nothing new under the sun.

10 Men may say of something,
"Look, this is new!"

But the same thing existed long
ago before our time.

11 For the men of today do not
remember yesterday, just as the
men of tomorrow will not
remember today.

Oh, what miserable futility God himself has subjected the family of man to!

12 I, Ecclesiastes, was king over Israel in Jerusalem.
13 And I completely gave myself over to observing and investigating, with the use of wisdom, everything that is done under the sun.

14 I have seen all the works that are done under the sun, and behold, all is vanity and chasing the wind,
15 a crookedness that cannot be straightened, an emptiness that cannot be filled.

16 Then I said to myself, "Well now, having put wisdom and knowledge to such use, I have nevertheless accumulated more wisdom than anyone before me in Jerusalem."

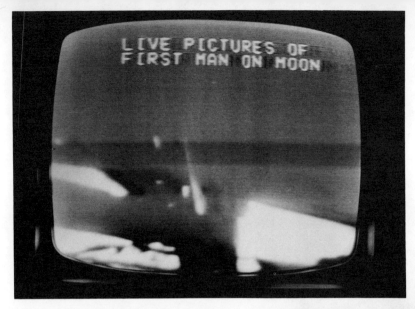

17 But when I gave my heart over to wisdom and knowledge as ends in themselves, they became madness and folly and I saw that they too are like chasing the wind.

18 For in much wisdom is much grief, and he who increases knowledge increases sorrow.

2:1 I then said to myself, "So I will experiment in pleasure and try 'living it up.'" But this also turned out to be just another futility.

2 Laughter, I concluded, is mere foolishness; and as for pleasure, what does it accomplish?

3 While still devoted in my heart to obtaining wisdom, I tried the stimulation of wine and the life of frivolity—all in the hope of seeing what is best for men to do during their few days of life under the sun.

4 I made great works. I built mansions and planted vineyards for myself.

5 I laid out gardens and parks in which I planted all kinds of fruit trees;

6 I made pools from which to water the forest of growing trees.

7 I bought male and female slaves and had slaves who were born in my house.

I acquired great possessions, more cattle and flocks than any of my predecessors in Jerusalem.

8 I amassed silver and gold equal to the treasures of many kings.

I kept both men and women entertainers, and also the special delight of men—mistresses, many of them.

9 Greater and richer I grew, more than anyone before me in Jerusalem; nor did my wisdom leave me.

10 Whatever my eyes desired, I refused them nothing; nor did I deny myself any pleasure.

And indeed I derived pleasure from all my labor, and pleasure was my endeavor's reward.

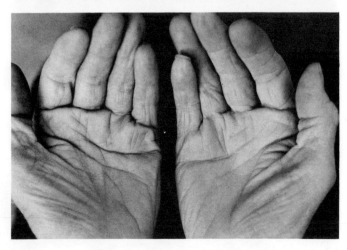

11 But when I looked at all my hands had achieved, and thought of all the time and effort these achievements had cost, it was clear that all of it was emptiness and grabbing at the wind. For there is no value that lasts under the sun.

12 So once again I began to reflect on the madness and folly of wisdom. For what more could anyone do than I, the king, had already done—unless it would be to repeat the same futile achievements?

13 I am sure the teaching is true that "Wisdom is better than folly as light is better than darkness"; and,

14 "The wise man sees ahead, but the fool walks in darkness."

And yet I saw that the very same fate will finally come to both of them.

15 So I asked myself, "Since I shall come to the same fate as the fool, why is my wisdom such an advantage?" And thus I concluded that wisdom too is ultimately futile.

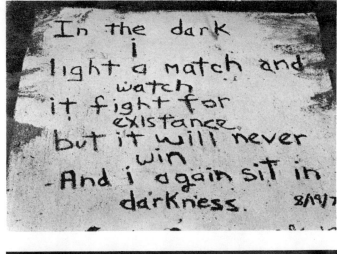

In the dark
i
light a match and
watch
it fight for
existance
but it will never
win
-And i again sit in
darkness.   8/19/7

16 For the wise man is remembered no longer than the fool, since I see that as the passing days multiply, both are soon forgotten. And how does the wise man die?—in exactly the same way as the fool!

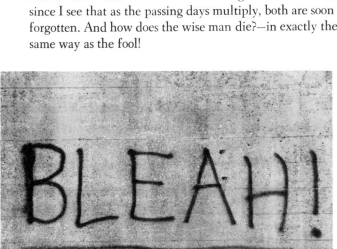

17 So I came to hate life, for all the work done under the sun seemed pointless to me, and everything futile and chasing the wind.

18 I also came to hate all that I had achieved under the sun, seeing that I would have to leave it to someone who comes after me.

19 For, on the one hand, who knows whether this "someone" will be wise or foolish? And yet everything I have achieved by much wisdom and work will be at his disposal. This also is vanity.

20 I also fell into despair about all that I had achieved under the sun,
21 because, on the other hand, a man who has worked with wisdom and knowledge
and skill must leave all of the fruit of his labor to someone who has *not* worked for it.
Surely this also is meaningless and a great injustice.

22 So what does a man finally gain then by all
his work and effort and struggle under the
sun?

23 For all his days are spent in grief and
trouble.

Even in the night his mind is restless. This
also is vanity.

24 There is nothing better for a man than to eat and drink and find enjoyment in doing his work.

This, I came to see, is a gift from the hand of God,
25 since both enjoyment and lack of enjoyment come from God's own will.

26 For God gives wisdom and knowledge and enjoyment to whomever he pleases; but to another man God gives the task of gathering possessions which are then only to be handed over to whomever God wishes. This also is incomprehensible and like chasing the wind.[15]

3:1 There is a fixed time for everything; a predestined hour for everything that occurs under the sun.[16]

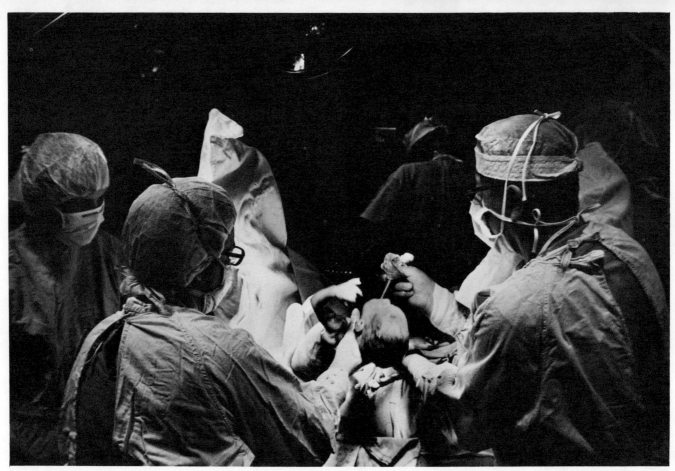

2 A time of birth,

and a time of death;

A time of sowing,

and a time of reaping what has been sown;

3 A time of killing,

and a time of healing;

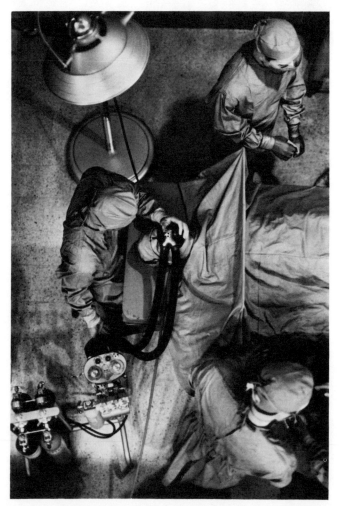

A time of breaking down,

and a time of building up;

4 A time of weeping,

and a time of laughing;

A time of mourning,

and a time of dancing for joy;

5 A time of casting away stones,[17]

and a time of gathering stones together;

A time of embracing,

and a time of shunning embraces;

6 A time of seeking,

and a time of surrendering;

A time of keeping,

and a time of setting free;

7 A time of tearing,

and a time of mending;

A time of silence,

and a time of speech;

8 A time of love,

and a time of hate;

A time of war,

and a time of peace.

9 What then does the doer of any of these things add by his own will and effort?

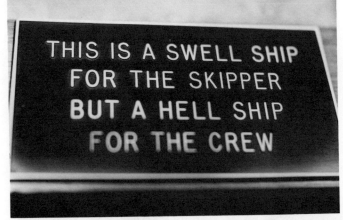

10 I have seen the frustration that God has subjected mankind to:

11 God has made everything good in its time;[18]

yet at the same time, God has put questions of eternity into men's hearts, but in such a way that men cannot know the answer to what God's overall purpose may be from the beginning to the end.

12 I know therefore that there is nothing better for men than pleasure and enjoying life while they live.

13 Indeed, when a man can eat and drink and find pleasure in his toil, this is a gift from God.

14 I know that whatever God does is unchangeable; nothing can be added to it, nor anything subtracted from it. God alone brings all things about in order that men should humbly fear him.

15 Whatever is and whatever is to be have already been predetermined; and God never relinquishes control of his creation.

16 Nevertheless, I observed that under the sun there is wickedness where righteousness and justice should be.

17 I said to myself, "God will judge the righteous and the wicked, for there is with God an appointed time for every intention and every deed."

Memento from Auschwitz, Nazi Concentration Camp, 1943-1945.

18 In this behavior of men, I reflected, God is limiting them in order to show them their own finitude and their bestial behavior to each other.

19 For man is controlled by fate exactly as animals are controlled by fate; and one final
   fate awaits them both—death! They both draw the same breath of life; and man's
   advantage over other beasts is nothing, for all is a breath that vanishes.

20 All are bound for the same
   destination: all are from the dust and
   all return to dust again.

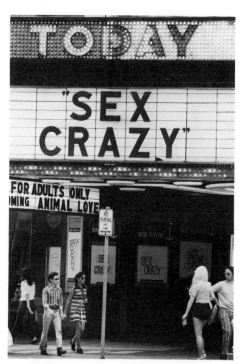

21 Who knows whether the spirit of
   man goes upward and the animal's
   spirit goes down to the earth?

22 Therefore I saw that there is nothing better for a man than to enjoy what he is now doing, since this is his lot.

For who can enable him to see what lies beyond his life?

4:1 Then I observed all the oppression that is practiced under the sun. I saw the tears of the oppressed who have no one to comfort them. Their oppressors have power in their hands, but the downtrodden themselves have no avenger.

2 I concluded that the dead, those already in their graves, are more fortunate than the living who are still alive.

3 But better off than either of these is the person
  not yet born, who has never seen the evil that is
  done under the sun.

4 Then I saw that all effort and all
  achievement come from men's
  envy of their fellow men. This
  also is vanity and grasping for
  the wind.

5 It is a fool who folds his hands and lets his own
  flesh waste away.

6 Nevertheless, one handful with contentment is better than two handfuls achieved by toiling and grasping for the wind.

I'M TOO BUSY TO HAVE TIME FOR ANYTHING IMPORTANT.

7 Then I saw still another example of futility under the sun:
8 a man with no family at all, but toiling ceaselessly for riches he never obtained, did not stop even long enough to ask himself, "If my work is depriving me of contentment, for whom then am I working so hard?" This kind of thing also is vanity and an empty busyness.

I NEED SOME ONE

+ DEB   DONNA ARVIN M.W.

9 Two are better than one. They get a better return from their work.
10 For if one falls, the other can lift his companion up again.

But woe to those who fall and are alone, and have no one to lift them up.

11 Further, if two sleep together, they keep each other
   warm. But how can one keep warm alone?

12 Whereas someone alone may be overcome by an
   enemy, two together can resist.

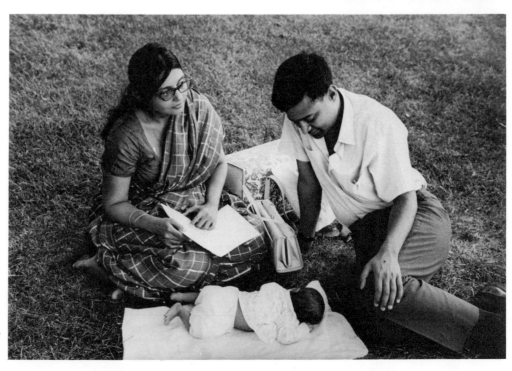

And a three-ply cord is not easily
broken.

13 As it is said, "Better is a poor but wise youth than an old and foolish king"—like the one who no longer knew how to heed warnings.

14 The youth may have risen to the throne in a popular rebellion, even though he was born poor in the land he would later rule.

15 I watched all the living under the sun throng to such a young man who was to replace the old king; no end of people hailed him as their leader.

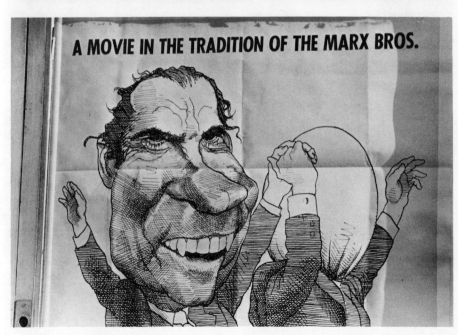

16 And yet this same man will turn out to be very unpopular later on. This is still another example of futility and running after the wind.

5: 1 Be extremely cautious when you go to the house of God. Drawing near to learn in fear and humble receptiveness is better...

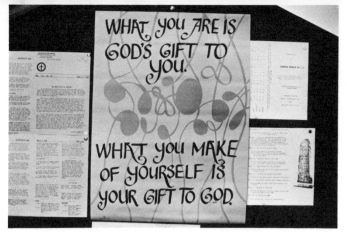

...than the fools who come, believing they can give a gift to God so that God will then owe them something. They do not even know that they are doing evil.[19]

2 Be careful that your heart is not hasty nor your mouth glib when you speak in God's presence.

For God is in heaven and you are on earth. Therefore let your words be few.

3 For as much activity produces delusions of one's own greatness, much speaking produces the voice of a fool.

4 If you make a vow to God, fulfill your promise faithfully; for God is not pleased by fools. Make good what you have vowed.

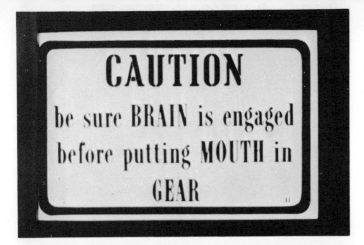

5 Better is no vow at all than vowing and failing to fulfill it.

6 Do not say anything that is irresponsible in God's sight. Nor by claiming, "I didn't mean it!", do not expect to right your wrong to the angel who will come to judge you later. Why let careless speech anger God, who can destroy everything you have worked for?

7 For great opinions of oneself produce great numbers of thoughtless words. Therefore, fear God!

8 If in some land you see oppression of the poor and violation of justice and people's rights, do not be surprised.

For high officials are looked down on by even higher officials. And over all of them the king is watching.

9 Nevertheless, this desire of men to lord it over other men, if wisely controlled, can be made to work for the common good.[20]

10 He who loves money will not be satisfied with money; nor will he who loves riches be satisfied with what money can buy: this also is vanity.

11 When wealth increases, so do the parasites who live off it.

And what advantage are great riches to their owner? Since he obviously cannot eat them, what good are they except to be looked at?

12 The laboring man's sleep is sweet regardless of how much he eats.

But the rich man's wealth will not allow him to sleep.

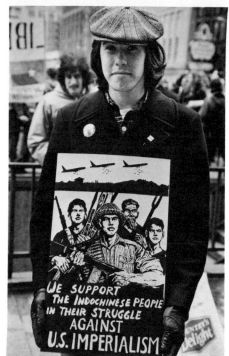

13 A painful misfortune I have seen under the sun is this—great wealth was protected by its owner to his hurt.

14 And when that wealth was lost through a bad mistake, he had nothing left of any value to pass along to his son.

15 Just as he came from his mother's womb, so he will also go—naked as he came. There will not be a single result of any of his labor that he can take with him.

16 Just think of the calamity! He will leave life exactly as he arrived—with nothing. And what has he gained by all of his toiling for the wind in the meantime?

17 All his days are spent in the shadows of deep anxiety and grief, sickness and resentment.

18 This, then, is my conclusion: It is good and proper for a man to eat and drink and be content with all the work he has to do under the sun, during the few days God gives him to live; for this is man's lot.

19 Furthermore, every man to whom God gives wealth and possessions and power to enjoy them, and to accept his lot and find contentment in his toil—this man has a special gift from God.

20 At least such a man will not need to brood over the brevity of life, because God is thus keeping his mind occupied with pleasant thoughts.

6: 1 There is an evil under the sun that I observe weighing men down—it is this:

2 Consider the man to whom God gives wealth, riches and honor, so that he lacks nothing he could possibly desire. If God does not also give him the power to enjoy these things, but a stranger is destined to enjoy them, this is a sad misfortune and a great futility.

3 A man may father a hundred children and live many years; but regardless of how plentiful his days may be, if this man does not find contentment in life—I say that a stillborn child is better off than he.

4 A stillborn's coming is completely futile: it arrives in darkness and departs in darkness, never even given a name and with little or no funeral.[21]

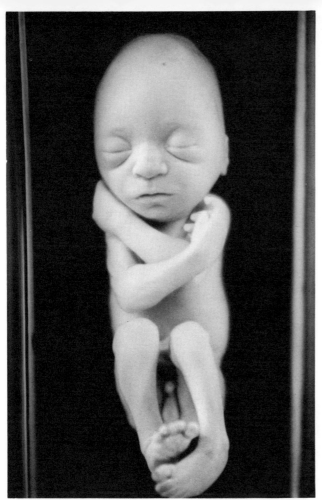

5 But even though a stillborn never sees the sun or knows anything, its lot is happier than his.

6 For even if a man should live a thousand years twice over, but find no contentment—has not the stillborn's been the easiest way to the same destination?

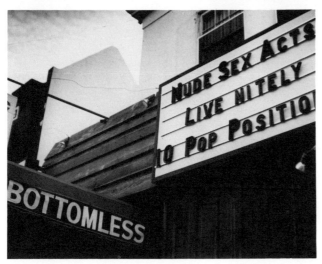

7 Everything a man does is to fill up his own desires, but, alas, his desires remain bottomless.

8 So what advantage then does a wise man have either over a fool or over a poor man who nevertheless knows how to find contentment in life?

9 Satisfaction with what can be seen is better than getting carried away by dreams. This, too, is futile and like chasing the wind.

10 Whatever happens was predestined long ago. Indeed man's destiny itself was long ago foreknown and he cannot dispute with One mightier than he.

11 The more man tries to dispute this, the more ludicrous such an effort becomes. And what does man gain by that?

12 For who knows what is good for man while he lives the few days of his futile existence which he passes like a shadow? For who can tell him what will follow after his time under the sun?

7:1 A good reputation in life is sweeter than the finest ointment; therefore the day of one's death is more important than the day of one's birth.

2 It is better to go to a funeral than to a party; for death is the end of all men, and the living should keep this in mind.

3 Grief is better than laughter, because difficulties on the outside produce a deeper wisdom inside.

4 Therefore wise men's thoughts are at home with death and mourning, while fools prefer the frivolous.

5 It is better to listen to the reprimands of the wise...

...than to the pleasantries of fools.

6 For like the sound and fury of blazing thistles under a kettle, so is the laughter of fools—both amount to a puff of smoke.

7 Nevertheless, excessive sorrow can drive mad even the wise; and temptation can seduce the noblest heart.

8 The conclusion of a thing is more important than its beginning; therefore patience is better than pride.

9 Be careful in letting yourself become angry; for the heart mastered by anger is the heart of a fool.

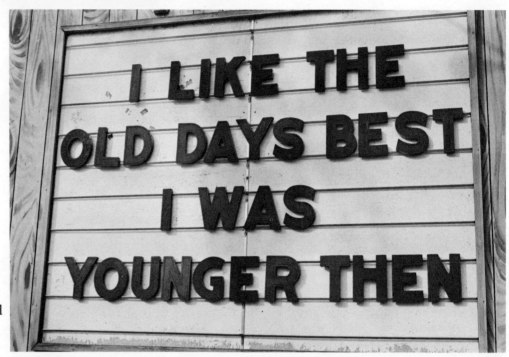

10 Do not ask, "What happened to the good old days?" A wise man will not ask such a question.

11 Having wisdom is like having an inheritance; it is an advantage to men while they see the sun.

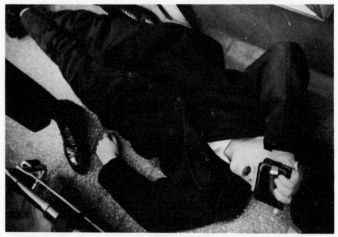

12 For being protected by wisdom is like being protected by money; but wisdom is better than money—it is a better safeguard of a man's life.

13 Consider the work of God: Who can straighten what he has made crooked?

14 When life is sweet, enjoy it; but when life is hard, remember this: God has brought about the one as well as the other in order to prevent man from finding any created thing completely trustworthy.

15 During the fleeting days of my life I have seen everything— from a righteous man being destroyed because of his righteousness to a wicked man thriving on his wickedness.

16 Therefore do not be overrighteous or overwise. Why should you let this destroy you?

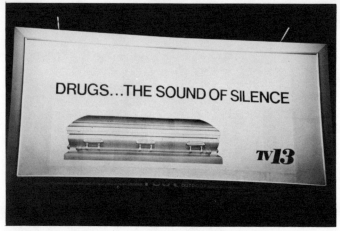

17 But neither be overwicked nor a fool. Why should you die before your time?

18 The best course is never to commit oneself totally to any one thing; for he who fears God will place his complete trust in nothing else.

19 Wisdom gives more strength to a man than ten rulers can give to a city.

20 And yet there is no virtuous man on earth who, even while doing good, is ever free from sin.

21 Do not pay too much attention to everything men say, or you will hear your own servant cursing you.

22 And you know full well how many times you yourself have cursed others.

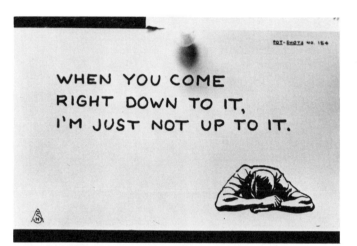

23 I came to all these conclusions by means of wisdom, thinking I was myself quite wise. But true wisdom does not lie within me.

24 The fundamental wisdom behind all practical wisdom lies beyond our grasp; it is deep, so very deep, that who can lay his hands upon the heart of things?

25 With all my heart I attempted to question and to search for wisdom and for the reason behind things, only to find that it is folly to be wicked and insanity to act like a fool.

26 More bitter than death itself were my experiences with women. Woman's heart is a steel trap and her arms are chains. By God's favor one may escape her; but whomever God disapproves will be caught by her.

27 In vain I have again and again tried to get to the heart of things, thinking things through one after another.

28 But I have observed this, says Ecclesiastes: I have found only one true man in a thousand, and among women I have found none at all.

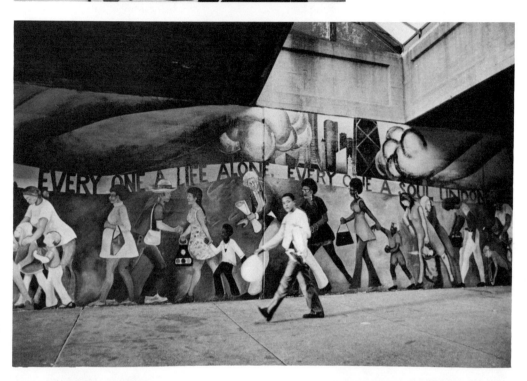

29 Therefore, I have only been able to conclude this: God created man for Himself, but men are given to inventing many false gods.[22]

:1 Who is like the wise man? Who else knows how to interpret things? Wisdom brightens a man's face; the hardness of his countenance is transformed.

2 Keep the king's command, especially when the king is God himself.

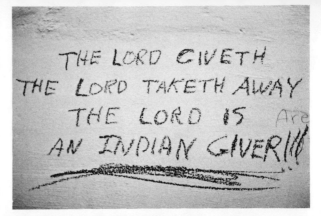

3 Do not rebel against him, nor do not hesitate to obey if his demand is unpleasant. For the king does as he pleases.

4 Since the king is himself the highest authority, who can say to him, "What is your authority for doing that?"

5 He who obeys the command will avoid trouble, for the wise man knows there will be a time of judgment.

6 But though there is a time of judgment for everything, man is still greatly troubled
7 by ignorance of what the future finally holds; for who can tell man what will ultimately happen?

8 No man has power to control the spirit or authority over the day of death.

No man can escape from this war between life and death.

Nor can a wicked man free himself from being wicked.

9 All these things I saw as I applied my mind to everything that is done "under the sun"—the place of man's tyranny over his fellow man.

10 I have seen pompous funerals for evil men; and as their mourners returned from the "holy services," these same evil men were praised in the very cities where they had committed their villainies. This is just one more example of vanity.

11 Because judgment against evil deeds is slow in coming, men's hearts are encouraged to do evil.

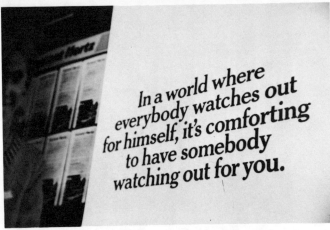

12 But though a sinner does wrong a hundred times and even prolongs his life, still I know it will be better for those who fear God, precisely because they fear him.

13 On the other hand, it will not be well with the wicked man; for even if he does prolong his days, they will be—because he does not fear God—as empty as a shadow.

14 Nevertheless, there is this great puzzle on earth: The best men can have the worst luck, and the worst men can have the best luck. This indeed is meaningless![23]

15 Therefore, I praise enjoyment, since there is no other good for man under the sun but to eat and drink and be merry; this is the only sure thing of value that can accompany man as he struggles through the days of his life that God has given him under the sun.

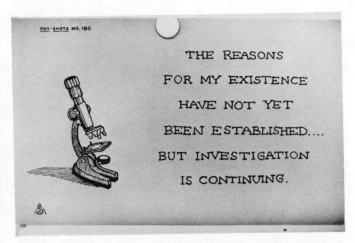

16 When I gave myself over to wisdom and observing all the activity taking place on earth, I saw that although man's eyes may never close in sleep,

17 still he will not be able to see the purpose God has behind his rule of the world.

No matter how much a man may struggle to discover this purpose, he will not be able to find it.

And even though a wise man claims to know it, he will never get to the truth of it.

9:1 This I saw and clearly understood: That the righteous and the wise and all that they do are controlled by God's hand. But whether behind this control there is love or hate—no man knows.

All things come to all men from a source beyond their control, just as the same fate can come to any two men—to the innocent and the guilty, to the good and the evil, to the pure and the impure, to the one who sacrifices and the one who does not sacrifice, to the good man and the sinner, to the one who swears and the one who refuses to swear.

3 The evil that overshadows everything done under the sun is this: All men are in the same predicament—the hearts of men are full of evil ...

...madness fills their hearts while they live...

...and then they go down to the dead.

4 But only the living have any hope; and therefore a living dog is better than a dead lion.

5 At least the living know that they will die, but the dead know nothing at all. Nor does anything good come to the dead. They are utterly gone *and* forgotten.

6 Their loves, their hates, their jealousies, are all stopped short; nor will they ever again take part in anything done under the sun.

7 Go to it then, eat your food with enjoyment, and drink your wine with a merry heart; for it is God's good pleasure that you find enjoyment while you live.

8 Always wear the clothes of happiness and do not stint on sweet-smelling oil for your head.

I need you to help me enjoy my loneliness

9 Enjoy life with a woman you love, all the days of your life that God gives you under the sun, fleeting and purposeless as they are. For enjoyment is all we are meant to get out of life as we go on toiling under the sun.

TIME IS RUNNING OUT

10 Whatever you put your hand to, do it with all your might. For there is no doing nor thinking nor understanding nor wisdom in the grave to which you are going.

Nice guys finish last

WHEEL FORTUNE

11 I also saw under the sun that races are not won by the swift, nor battles by the strong; nor does bread come to the wise, nor wealth to the intelligent, nor recognition to the gifted. For all things are governed by time and chance.

12 And man no more knows his own time of mischance than fish caught in the fatal net or birds trapped in a snare. Thus men are also victims of misfortune when it suddenly overtakes them.

13 Also, I was greatly impressed by this example of evil I saw under the sun:

14 There was a small town with only a few men in it; and a great king attacked and surrounded it, and built great siegeworks against it.

15 In this town there was a poverty-stricken wise man who managed to save the entire town by his wisdom. But afterward no one remembered this poor man.

16 Nevertheless, I say that wisdom is better than might, even if a poor man's wisdom is completely ignored and his words go unheeded.

17 A wise man speaking his mind quietly is better than a commander shouting orders among fools.

18 Wisdom is better than weapons of war, but a single fool can undo much good.

10: 1 As one poisonous fly can cause the perfumer's ointment to stink, so can a grain of folly mar much wisdom and honor.

2 A wise man's heart will lead him aright, but a fool's heart leads him astray.

3 When a fool looks around at the world, his lack of understanding causes him to think everyone else is foolish.

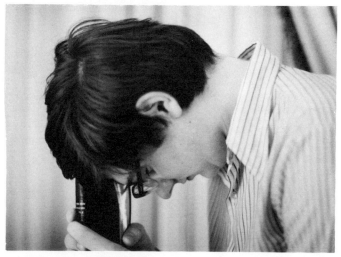

4 If the ruler becomes angry with you, do not hastily leave your post, but humbly submit to him and you will make amends for great offenses.

5 Here is another evil I have seen here under the sun, a folly for which those who govern are often responsible:

6 Fools are placed in high offices while the noble are given insignificant jobs.

7 I have seen base men riding fine horses, while the truly noble plod about on foot like slaves.

8 All of man's work has its pitfalls: Those who break down walls may be bitten by a snake;

9 those who quarry stones may be injured by a stone; and woodcutters must be careful in chopping down trees.

10 If a knife is dull and not sharpened beforehand, its use will require more effort. Likewise a sharp-witted man has a better chance of success.

11 If a snake bites someone before it has been charmed, what is the use then of a snake charmer?

12 A wise man's words will win him favor, but a fool's words will lead to his own undoing.

13 Although he begins by talking mere nonsense, he will end in mad mischief.

14 Though a fool thinks he knows it all, no man really knows what will happen in the future. For who can say what is going to be after us?

15 The fool is exhausted by his efforts, because he does not even set out in the right direction.

16 It bodes ill for you, O country with a young king, where princes party until morning.

17 But happy is the country whose princes eat at a respectable hour to give themselves strength and not to make themselves drunk.

18 For where men are lazy,
the roof sinks in. Where
men are undisciplined,
the house leaks.

19 "But," they say, "a party is made for laughter, wine
gladdens the heart, and money will take care of
everything."

20 If you cannot avoid thinking them altogether, keep your
evil thoughts to yourself about the king and the rich.
For "a little bird" may repeat what you say. Indiscretions
have a way of sprouting wings.

11:1 On the other hand, scatter your nourishing bread upon
the waters—far and wide and indiscriminately. For good
has a way of coming from good even after many days.

2 Invest the means you have in several ventures, for who
knows when or where disaster will strike in this life?

3 When will it rain? When the clouds become full! Where will a fallen tree lie? In the direction the wind knocks it down!

4 Furthermore, anyone who spends his time watching the wind and the clouds will neither sow nor reap.

5 And just as you cannot know what direction the wind will take, or the mysteries of a child in its mother's womb, so you cannot know what is in the mind of God, who does all.

6 Therefore sow your seed in the morning, and in the evening do not stop your hands. For you can never know which attempt will succeed, whether this one or that one, or whether both will turn out well.

7 Truly light is sweet! And it is
  pleasant for the eyes to see the sun.
8 And therefore if a man lives many
  years, let him enjoy all of them.

For let him remember that the
days of darkness will be many.
All that is to come is emptiness.

9 Therefore, rejoice in your youth, O young man, and let your heart be cheerful in the days of your youth. Let your heart and your eyes show you the way. But also be sure of this: God will judge whether you have made good use of all he has given you.

10 Therefore, remove sadness from your heart and do not let your body suffer pain. For your childhood and youth will soon pass away.

12: 1 Remember also your Creator in the days of your youth, before the evil days come and the years steal upon you when you will say, "My days give me no pleasure."

2 Remember him before the light from the sun and the moon and the stars grow dim, and the rain is followed by even darker clouds;

3 In the days when the keepers of the house tremble, And the strong men are bent,

And the grinders are idle because they are few, and day is darkening at the windows;

4 When the doors to the street are shut, and the sound of the mill is faint;

And one awakens when the first bird chirps;

And all the daughters of song are barely audible;

5 When to walk uphill is an ordeal, and one is terrified of falling down;

When the hair is as white as an almond tree in blossom,

And one drags oneself along like a grasshopper,

And even the stimulants for desire are useless.

For all men are on their way
to their long, long home;

And the mourners are
already waiting.

6 Remember him before the silver cord is cut, and the golden bowl falls and is broken;

Before the pitcher is shattered at the spring, and the wheel is broken at the well;

7 Before the dust returns to the earth as it was, and the breath of life returns to God who gave it.

8 Futile, empty, and meaningless! says Ecclesiastes. Fleeting, incomprehensible, and pointless! All things are vanity.

9 And so Ecclesiastes, in his wisdom, continued to teach the people knowledge, testing and amending and fashioning many proverbs with great care.

10 Ecclesiastes tried to find pleasing ways to express the honest truth.

11 For the sayings of the wise are like sharp goads; like firmly fixed nails are all the sayings that come from the One Shepherd.

12 Furthermore, my son, beware of going beyond what has here been said. For there is no end to all the books that are made, and much study will wear one's strength away.

13 Listen carefully now to the conclusion of the whole matter: Fear God, and obey his commandments! For this is the whole duty of man.

14 For God brings everything we do—even the hidden things—into judgment of whether they are good or evil.

II

Ecclesiastes: Of All the Bible's Books, the Truest for Us Today

To everything, turn, turn, turn,
There is a season, turn, turn, turn,
And a time to every purpose under heaven.

. . . .

A time to gain, a time to lose;
A time to rend, a time to sew;
A time of love, a time of hate;
A time of peace, I swear it's not too late.
> —"Turn! Turn! Turn! To Everything
> There Is a Season," by Pete Seeger, 1968

We can know precious little about God from the world in which we live; it gives us very little help towards any kind of experience of God. We no longer discover, like the psalmist, the marks of God in nature, and we no longer see, like the prophets, the great acts of God in history. For this reason it is such writings as the book of . . . Ecclesiastes . . . which we are able to accept as prophecies of Christ, rather than the mighty prophetic oracles which are read in church at Advent and Christmas. When we look at the reality round about us, our first impression is of a world which is obscure and opaque; we sense an irreconcilable discord in existence, in which the scales are tilted towards the darkness.

This is also the reason why the sceptical observations of Ecclesiastes have once become so relevant. Although the Preacher lived more than two thousand years ago, he seems to us almost like a contemporary. When he looks at the world, he, too, perceives little in it which tells him of God. All he finds in it is contradictions, which do not fit in with God. He cannot pile up enough contradictory concepts to describe the ambiguity of existence:

> A time to be born, and a time to die; a time to plant, and a time to pluck up what is planted; a time to kill, and a time to heal; a time to break down, and a time to build up; a time to weep, and a time to laugh; a time to mourn, and a time to dance; . . . a time to love, and a time to hate; a time for war, and a time for peace.

All these contradictions he finds not following each other or accompanying each other, providing a meaningful solution to one or complementing each other, but confused and entangled with each other, entwined with each other in a meaningless way, cutting across and destroying each other in mutual hostility, apparently without end. The world he describes is enigmatic, discordant and contradictory —it is the world in which we live. But where is God in it?

—Heinz Zahrnt, *What Kind of God?* 1971[1]

Into the mike that is there no bigger than a lollipop [Babe] begins to sing, sings in a voice that is no woman's voice at all and no man's, is merely human, the words of Ecclesiastes. A time to be born, a time to die. A time to gather up stones, a time to cast stones away. Yes. The Lord's last word. There is no other word, not really.

—John Updike, *Rabbit Redux,* 1971[2]

A. ECCLESIASTES AND MODERN MAN: MEN OF THE SAME BASIC QUESTION

The deep and widespread fascination men have had for Ecclesiastes is a perennial one. Indeed it is this very fascination that has helped to explain, for some, how such an "unorthodox" and "worldly" book came to be numbered among the books of the Bible in the first place. In spite of "its unconventional character," says Old Testament scholar Robert Gordis, "the book must have exercised an undeniable fascination upon the people and their spiritual leaders, as evidenced by their unwillingness to surrender it."[3] But this original fascination was only the beginning of Ecclesiastes' perpetual appeal. "In every age," says Gordis, "men have sought the key to the understanding of this modern classic, which accidentally happened to be written two millennia ago. There will be times when it will not suit the temper of the age, but it will never be outmoded as long as the systole and diastole of human life survives, and men fluctuate between progress and reaction, growth and decline, hope and disillusion."[4] The explanation for Ecclesiastes' enduring attraction lies in the fact that, as very few works have, it has given perfect utterance to a deep and universal human need, the need for a satisfactory Answer in the face of life's hardest Question: What is the *meaning* of life? And thus Ecclesiastes unites us in that he, like the rest of mankind, is much clearer about life's Question than about its Answer. "Community in the form of answers always turns out to be divisive and partisan," says theologian Jürgen Moltmann. "But the community of open questions affords a universal solidarity among men who have nothing of their own, except perhaps the hope sometime to find an answer."[5]

And although it may be true that Ecclesiastes has spoken more relevantly to some ages than to others, and yet with a certain startling directness to all ages, there is no doubt that Ecclesiastes is alive and well in the hearts and minds of twentieth-century man. He "speaks to the modern age . . . with the immediacy of contact of a contemporary" (Gordis).[6] From the section of Ecclesiastes read while most of the United States watched the televised funeral of John F. Kennedy (verses 3:1-8 were among the assassinated President's favorite passages from Scripture), to "the songs the kids are singing," to the latest Updike novel, on down to the recent best-selling *The Savage God—A Study of Suicide,* the words and name of Ecclesiastes seem to pop up everywhere. What is more important, even if we do not know his puzzling name or strangely haunting words, the attitude and outlook of "Koheleth," or "The Preacher," as he is sometimes called, are definitely ours: "The spirit of the Preacher is strong today in our minds. His mood fills our philosophy and poetry. The vanity of human existence is described powerfully by those who call themselves philosophers or poets of existence. They all are the children of the Preacher, this great existentialist of his period" (Paul Tillich).[7] Ecclesiastes has aptly been described as "the most modern book in the Bible." But why is he so close, so true to our age in particular? Surely part of the reason lies in the fact that, more than ever before, modern man has been driven back on himself to answer the same stark *question* Ecclesiastes was forced to face with such brutal honesty. We are both like Alex, the young anti-hero in Anthony Burgess' novel *A Clockwork Orange*: our eyelids clamped open, we are forced to watch a never-ending film of human depravity and "ultra-violence" until we gag and retch and "creech" for help. Ecclesiastes and modern men do not merely *smell* "the vanity of human existence"; their noses are rubbed in it. "There has been since the beginning of the twentieth century a growing interest . . . in Ecclesiastes," says Old Testament professor G. G. Atkins, "some of it due to the literary charm of the book. But most of all because Koheleth's amazing modernity has a way of reasserting itself and its kinship with the time and spirit of a world war-worn, disillusioned, and weary."[8]

Disillusionment and world-weariness are indeed the stuff modern men and Ecclesiastes are both made of. The biblical scholars are agreed: "Part of the fascination of the work is that the climate of opinion out of which it grew has come back in our own day. Older certainties have crumbled and we look, some despairingly, for value and meaning" (Edgar Jones).[9] But there are still two other reasons why the shock of recognition is so strong when we moderns read the Preacher's words today. His *question* is ours—yes. But in addition, his *method* for finding an answer to this question is also "surprisingly up-to-date" (F. N. Jasper),[10] as are likewise many of his *conclusions*.

B. ECCLESIASTES AND MODERN MAN: MEN OF SIGHT, SECULARIZATION AND THE SCIENTIFIC METHOD

The secular spirit of both Ecclesiastes and modern man has the same source—the deity of the God of the Old Testament. For when this God is seriously believed to be the Creator, the "Wholly Other," a "jealous" God who alone shall be worshiped and served, a necessary consequence of this belief will be that the creation itself—the world and all that is in it—is deprived of any divinity attaching to it. The divinity of God means the "dedivinization," the disenchanting, the "desacralization" of everything else. "If we have faith in God we are no longer slaves of the gods," says German physicist Carl F. von Weizsäcker. "God himself has deprived the world of its divinity."[11] According to theologian Karl Barth, the monotheism with which ancient Israel "invaded Palestine was the radical dedivinisation of nature, history and culture—a remorseless denial of any other divine presence . . . "; and therefore to the "Canaanites . . . the God of Israel must have appeared . . . as death incarnate, and the faith of Israel as irreligion itself."[12]

The result of all this divesting of nature of any magical power is that all things become nondivine, natural things, available for man's examination and study. On the basis of this belief in God, man can fearlessly investigate anything in the world and put it to his own use and enjoyment. This is why, in the New Testament, St. Paul can say to the Christian community that "all things are yours" (1 Cor. 3:21). In other words, "God is in heaven," as Ecclesiastes says; and for those who seriously believe that this God *alone* is God, the demonic pseudo-divinities of superstition and magic are driven out of all creation and man can freely go about his God-appointed task, given to him in the very first chapter of the Bible, to "Be fruitful and multiply, and fill the earth and subdue it" (Gen. 1:28). "When the principle of being is God," writes H. Richard Niebuhr, "then He alone is holy and ultimate sacredness must be denied to any special being. No special places, times, persons, or communities are more representative of the One than any others are. No sacred groves or temples, no hallowed kings or priests, no festival days, no chosen communities are particularly representative of Him in whom all things live and move and have their being."[13]

Thus we can see how the modern radical secularization of the world and its accompanying scientific spirit have been necessary results of the biblical faith in God's transcendent deity. It is true that progress toward this goal has met with many reverses and perversions along the way, not least of all from "religion" itself. But that the biblical faith in God is the source and continuing sponsor of this inevitable consequence, there can be no doubt. "Total secularisation has not simply come upon Christian faith in the modern age as a calamity from outside, but is rather the ultimate outcome of something inherent and essential in the attitude to the world of Christian faith itself" (Zahrnt).[14] Faith encourages the secularization of the world because this means the rout of all false gods. For it is only when false gods are shown to be the weak chaff that they are, that the God of the Bible becomes strong in men's lives. This is why Bonhoeffer, one of the earliest prophets of the Christian faith's stake in a secularized world, could say, "The world that has come of age is more godless, and perhaps for that very reason nearer to God, than the world before its coming of age."[15] Biblical faith means the liberation of man *from* the world, enabling him to assume confidently the responsibility of a mature son of God *for* the world—the responsibility to "subdue" the world for himself and his fellow men.

Ecclesiastes, more than any other biblical writer, is a modern man in his appreciation, or "celebration," of the world merely as world. For Ecclesiastes, the world is neither a god nor the home of gods; the world itself cannot save us. In this sense all the world is "vanity." But at the same time, all the world is *good* as it is God's gift to man for his use and enjoyment. For this reason Karl Barth, writing on "The Christian's Place in Society," can rely heavily on Ecclesiastes:

To perceive the *absolute vanity* of life under the sun in the light of the heavenly life of God is also to perceive its *relative potentiality*. . . . We shall go in and out in the fear of God without becoming servants of the idols: we shall go in and out in perfect liberty. . . . "There is nothing better for a man than he should eat and drink, and that he should make his soul enjoy good in his labor. This also I saw, that it is from the hand of God" (Eccles. 2:24). . . . We affirm life. . . . This is not worldly

wisdom. This is truth in Christ. This is the solid and fundamental Biblical perception of life.[16]

Taking this and other cues like it from Barth, a fundamental theological revolution has been brought about almost singlehandedly within the last two decades by Dietrich Bonhoeffer, a man whose most provocative thought is best known by such phrases as "world come of age," "religionless Christianity," and "the man for others"; and whose life is best known by his martyrdom on a hangman's gallows for conspiring to kill Hitler. It is no accident that Ecclesiastes occupies a central place in the development of Bonhoeffer's most revolutionary thinking. This is because Bonhoeffer felt that because of its basically "nonreligious" or "life-affirming" character, the Old Testament in general, and Ecclesiastes in particular, could help to establish a real "point of contact" between Christian faith and the secular world. And thus one of the foremost interpreters of Bonhoeffer's contribution to recent Christian thought, James Woelfel, can say:

Bonhoeffer's use of Ecclesiastes underlies his description of the "religionless" Christian: "By [Christian] this-worldliness I mean living unreservedly in life's duties, problems, successes and failures, experiences and perplexities. In so doing we throw ourselves completely into the arms of God. . . ." The mature Christian in the modern world does not turn his back on the life God has given him, but accepts it fully and responsibly from God's hand. The writer of Ecclesiastes, Bonhoeffer believes, witnessed to such a life, a life in which God "has made everything beautiful in its time" (Eccles. 3:11).[17]

Recent theological investigation has also noticed how much Ecclesiastes is a soul-brother of modern man because of the scientific realism of both. Ecclesiastes, writes Walther Eichrodt, "as none before him, completes the de-personalization of the natural order, and so comes closest to the modern conception of the laws of Nature. . . ."[18] In an article entitled " 'The Preacher' As Scientist," William Johnstone concludes "that in the thought of Koheleth, scientific and technological procedures are, as it were, canonised. Here it is recognised that scientific observation is a necessary undertaking for man's fuller appreciation of his surroundings both natural and social, if man is to be delivered from debilitating half-truths, superficial beliefs and dogging prejudices." To Ecclesiastes, says Johnstone, "the activity of observation is all-important."[19] The truth of this statement is confirmed by even the most casual acquaintance with Ecclesiastes. He is strictly a man of his *eyes*. "Then I saw" . . . "Then I observed" . . . "Then I perceived" are phrases that run like a refrain throughout the Preacher's book. Like modern man, then, Ecclesiastes also is a man of *sight*—his conclusions about life being based thoroughly on what he can *see* with his own eyes. It is this method of coming to conclusions about life that accounts for Ecclesiastes' "utterly secular form" (von Rad).[20] "So," concludes Paul Tillich, "if you meet people who attack Christianity for having too many illusions tell them that their attacks would be much stronger if they allied themselves with the book of the Preacher. The very fact that this book is a part of the Bible shows clearly that the Bible is a most realistic book."[21]

C. ECCLESIASTES AND MODERN MAN: MEN OF INSIGHT AND SIMILAR CONCLUSIONS, TRAPPED BY THEIR OWN EYES

What has just been said does not mean that Ecclesiastes and modern men are simply naïve, superficial "scientific realists" content with what their eyes can see. Their "realism" goes much deeper than that. With their eyes so sensitively sharpened, they sadly begin to see "through the thickness of things" (Kafka). Their sight becomes insight, and their wisdom begins to move in the direction of madness. For another characteristic held deeply in common by Ecclesiastes and modern man is what Camus called "that hopeless encounter between human questioning and the silence of the universe."[22] Just as modern

scientific man's confidence continues to waver because of the limitations of *his* vision (or "empiricism"), Ecclesiastes likewise had to come to some quick provisional conclusions but never found the Answer. What Old Testament theologian Gerhard von Rad has written of Ecclesiastes applies to modern man in a way that is too close for comfort:

It is a strange discovery! The despair of a wise man at a life which he knows to be completely encompassed by God, but which has nevertheless lost all meaning for him, because this God's activity has sunk down to unattainable concealment! The reason why this realisation is so devastating for Ecclesiastes is that he knows of no other possibility of coming into contact with God than this empirical way. But the world remains silent in face of his quest for salvation.[23]

The problem confronting Ecclesiastes is the *concealment* or *hiddenness* of God. His question is "What Kind of God?" Ecclesiastes is the Bible's clearest expression of that period in Israel's history which doubted God's "readiness to interfere drastically in history or in the life of the individual" (von Rad).[24] For Ecclesiastes this doubt resulted in a virtually *deistic* conception of the universe: God created the universe to resemble a new clock, wound it up and set it in motion, and then wandered off, apparently refusing to have anything more to do with it. Ecclesiastes was enough of a faithful child of Israel to know that God was the Creator of all —absolutely all—that is, and that he *continued* to be in complete control of his creation. At this point he had no doubts whatever. This firm belief in the deity only of God, as we have seen, in turn gave him the courage to use his head and eyes in investigating, "subduing" and enjoying the world. By virtue of his faith he was free from "bondage to beings that by nature are no gods . . . the weak and beggarly elemental spirits," to use St. Paul's words (Gal. 4:8-9). But ironically it was just this strong belief in God's *deity* that gave rise to his "deistic" view of the universe. Freed by God to use his head and eyes ("God has made everything good in its time . . ."), his head and eyes could tell him *nothing more* about the nature of God (". . . yet at the same time, God has put questions of eternity into men's hearts, but in such a way that men cannot know the answer to what God has done from the beginning to the end"— Eccles. 3:11). And thus Ecclesiastes sadly learns that "The eye is not satisfied with its seeing" (1:8). In the first place, what is life's meaning for man brought as he is into this seemingly indifferent, impersonal and mechanistic universe that God has created? Who knows? (6:12; 8:16-17.) Does God love us or hate us? Who knows? (9:1; 11:5.) Is there a future for man after death, and if so, what kind of future? From the beginning to the end the answer remains the same—No man knows! (3:21-22; 8:6-7; 10:14.) God's "Wholly Otherness," his transcendent deity and hiddenness, left Ecclesiastes with the conviction that very little could be said about what *kind* of God, God is: "God is in heaven and you are on earth; therefore let your words be few!" (5:2). Thus Ecclesiastes, trapped by his own eyes, is left only with an inscrutable "Clockwork God." Eichrodt's words quoted above, which seemed to contain such hope, now continue: Ecclesiastes "comes closest to the modern conception of the laws of Nature—except he sees this not indeed as a triumph but as a limitation of the human spirit thrown back on its own resources."

Here the *alien and incomprehensible quality of the cosmos* [says Eichrodt] has become so intensified that the regularity of its ordinances is no longer presented as an occasion for joy and wonder, but for "weariness," profound disillusionment and dejection. It seems no more than the running of a soulless piece of precision mechanism having no understandable purpose, nor any share in the sufferings and desires, the torments and hopes of mankind. (Eccles. 1:4 and following.) This is the "vanity" of the natural reading of the cosmic riddle.[25]

For Ecclesiastes, God is the great absentee, hidden in an impenetrable heaven, not only apparently careless of his creation but also in discord with it. The result of this view was the experience of meaninglessness or "vanity."

Modern man easily recognizes himself in this view of Ecclesiastes and its resulting experience because he is only one step removed from the same perspective. Whereas Ecclesiastes experiences meaninglessness in the face of a *concealed* God, modern man has the same experience in the face of a *nonexistent* God. In this respect modern man is truly a nihilist; his experience of meaninglessness is derived from his encounter with an utter void, with an absolute *nothing* in the heavens. For there is no denying that as a breed, modern man—even "religious" modern man—is an atheist. But today our atheism, or "godlessness," is no "big deal," as it has been in previous times. It is rather a deep, all-pervading assumption about life that we are not even conscious of. Just as often as not, it has all the outward appearances of "religiousness" and piety. For modern man, in *his* atheism, is simply "doing what comes naturally":

Whereas atheism was previously the concern of a small *avant-garde* group, it has now become a mass phenomenon. . . . It is not merely the theoretical view of a minority, but the unthinking practice of the majority. But although it has apparently become so superficial, it has at the same time put down much deeper roots. Atheism determines the intellectual and spiritual climate of our age; it is the air we breathe. It no longer constitutes a denial, but is an assertion in its own right. Nowadays people no longer come to atheism through what may be a severe inward struggle or through dangerous conflicts with society, but treat it as their automatic point of departure. . . . People are no longer concerned to refute God, but have passed beyond the problem of God.[26]

In today's atheism, modern man is the grandson of Ecclesiastes. The "old man" (most scholars agree that the author of Ecclesiastes was such), taking *his* "point of departure" from the belief that only the hidden God in heaven was God, thus arrived at a world which was only a world and devoid of any divinity of its own. His son, the Christian, inherited the old man's appreciation of the world as merely world, but also claimed to see in Christ the completed self-revelation of God that the old man had been looking for. The grandson, modern man, having become so thoroughly successful in exploiting his family's way of using its eyes, is now completely trapped by his eyes and fails to see—or find needful—anything of God anywhere. But in this self-reliant independence of the grandson, he suddenly turns into a remarkable likeness of the old man: trapped by his eyes, he becomes weary, disappointed and defiantly disgusted with the meaninglessness and ultimate futility of his life. The only difference being that whereas the old man finally had a faith—and therefore a hope—in God to fall back on, the grandson finally has only hopelessness. Whereas the grandfather held firmly to at least a "Clockwork *God*," the grandson now sees only a "Clockwork *Void*" staring him in the face. Such a situation is dreadful enough for both grandson *and* grandfather. But man cannot live by dread alone. Or, as T. S. Eliot was fond of saying, "Human kind cannot bear very much reality."[27]

D. ECCLESIASTES AND MODERN MAN: PARTNERS IN SEARCH OF LIFE'S GREATEST PLEASURE

Because of the dreadful reality that both Ecclesiastes and modern man are left facing, both are forced—they are literally "hell-bent"—to come up with an answer at least adequate enough to help them get through their respective nights. This answer, the solace they hold in common amidst the oppressive cosmic darkness surrounding them, is *pleasure,* or "enjoyment." If man's future on the other side of death is believed questionable, or denied altogether, what else is left for man except to fill up the little time allotted to him with whatever "pleasure" is available here and now? Thus here and now fulfill-

ment becomes the only hope available for man in an otherwise totally and meaningless absurd existence. It is for this reason that what has been said of Ecclesiastes also holds true for us moderns: his "counsel of joy as the highest good flows from a profoundly tragic conception of life."[28] And so when modern man says (in the words of the well-known ad), "You only go around once in life—so grab all the gusto you can!" he can find only bitter comfort in the fact that his soul-brother in the Bible agrees: "I saw that there is nothing better for a man than to enjoy what he is now doing, since this is his lot. For who can enable him to see what lies beyond his life?" (3:22). Barton sums up for Ecclesiastes (or "Qoheleth") the point which we have now reached:

His nature cries out for complete knowledge of the works of God, but God has doomed him to ignorance, so that the best he can do is to eat and drink and ignorantly get what little enjoyment he can within these limitations. . . . His philosophy of life, though in a sense hopeless, is not immoral. He nowhere counsels debauchery or sensuality; he rather shows that in these there is no permanent enjoyment. Though a sceptic, he had not abandoned his belief in God. It is true that God is for him no longer a warm personality or a being intimately interested in human welfare. . . . God is an inscrutable being. It is vain to seek to understand his works. All we can know is that he holds men in the iron vice of fate. Nevertheless Qoheleth preaches a gospel of healthy work and the full enjoyment of life's round of duties and opportunities. Let a man fulfill these while he bravely faces the real facts of life—this is the sum of Qoheleth's teaching.[29]

And so it is in "enjoyment" that Ecclesiastes "now sees one way open to him after all" (von Rad).[30] And in this "one way," which seeks the greatest pleasure life has to offer, Ecclesiastes again bears an uncanny resemblance to modern man. For nothing could be more obvious than the fact modern man takes his enjoyment with such grim seriousness that even his "play" has become full-time work. But one important question remains: *How* is this "greatest pleasure" to be found? It is in the answer to this question that Ecclesiastes and modern man at last part company. In this final split, however, Ecclesiastes is not left standing alone. For in his two-part answer, Ecclesiastes never leaves the mainstream of the biblical tradition—Old *and* New Testaments.

Pleasure Principle #1—Life's Greatest Pleasure Comes Only from Obedience to God Alone and from Nothing Else

In all the Old Testament there is no book more *prophetic* than Ecclesiastes. Although we will see that this statement is true in a twofold sense, here we are referring to "prophecy" in its "negative" or iconoclastic or "idol-smashing" mode. It is in this sense of prophecy that Walter Harrelson can write:

A crashing destruction of idols, of easy answers to the question of life's meaning—including religious answers—sounds throughout this book. We may therefore call the author another of Israel's great prophets.[31]

Israel's idea of an idol, or "false god," tended to be expressed in a way that sounds relatively harmless to modern ears—gods, for instance, "of wood and stone, the work of men's hands, that neither see nor hear, nor eat, nor smell" (Deut. 4:28). But in Ecclesiastes the means of expressing idolatry was broadened in a way which made it obvious that an idol could be—anything. For Ecclesiastes, as well as for the rest of the Bible, idolatry (or "sin") simply means centering all of one's hopes around *anything* that is *not* God. And because it is only *God* himself who is ever capable of fulfilling man's deepest "here-and-now" hopes and needs and desires, the result of a man's idolatry, or misdirected hopes, is always the same: the here-and-now experience of "vanity" or "futility" or "emptiness" or "grasping for the wind." In other words, "The results of idolatry is vanity" would be Ecclesiastes' way of

paraphrasing St. Paul's famous statement that "The wages of sin is death" (Rom. 6:23).

Our admiration for Ecclesiastes should be boundless! For in warning us about the illusory promises of false gods, he does not lecture us in vague abstractions received at second hand. This is why the unspecific word "idol" never even shows up in his book. Being the man of concrete experimentation that he was, Ecclesiastes has done us all the favor of personally plunging head-first off one deep end after another only to crawl back—battered and sadder, but wiser—to tell us that *"this* too is vanity." We might be amazed or amused that it took him so many hard tumbles against the concreteness of reality to get the point, but here again he is only a personification of everyone else's dullness in learning God's first —and really *only*—point: "You shall have no other gods besides me" (Ex. 20:3).

There are few things in which Ecclesiastes did *not* try to find life's greatest fulfillment. You name it—he tried it! "He searched the whole front of human existence—the wisdom sector; the power and possession sector; the sectors of self-indulgence and toil: and found nowhere any adequate balance between life's longings and its fugitive and shadowed harvests" (Atkins).[32] Although his eyes could not give him a clear picture of who God *is*, they served him well in showing him who God *is not*. Ecclesiastes, says Johnstone, "sets out deliberately to observe in an empirical way, leaving no area of life untouched. But the conclusion is that all is vanity, i.e. nothing observable is in the end valid, as giving the final truth about life, or as providing satisfaction, meaning or profit. This lies in God's gift alone."[33] One by one, each of the things in this world that men give their lives to—even including "righteousness"! (7:16)—is elevated or "idolized" by Ecclesiastes as an end in itself and is found sadly wanting. The inability of *anything finite* to provide men with a deep and abiding joy during their lives is a major theme upon which Ecclesiastes plays constant variations. "All things are vanity" is Ecclesiastes' alpha and omega, his beginning (1:2) and his end (12:8). And although no one has ever been more aware than Ecclesiastes that *death* will soon cancel any of life's little gains, his point is not simply that "you can't take it with you" or even that "it keeps slipping through your fingers while you're here!" For he is also very concerned to say that even if one *should* manage for his entire life to hang on to the "best" the world has to offer, this *too* would be "vanity" and basically unsatisfying: "It will not be well with the wicked man; for even if he does prolong his days, they will be—because he does not fear God—as empty as a shadow" (8:13).

Do these views of Ecclesiastes lead him then to a complete renunciation of everything finite, contemptuously shunning all worldly pleasures for a monk's vows of poverty and chastity? Quite the contrary! "The proper contempt of the world," said Luther in his commentary on Ecclesiastes (or "Solomon"), "is not that of the man who lives in solitude away from human society, nor is the proper contempt of gold that of the man who throws it away or who abstains from money, as the Franciscans do, but that of the man who lives his life in the midst of these things and yet is not carried away by his affection for them. This is the first thing that should be considered by those who are about to read Solomon."[34] Indeed it is this very ability to live life with such gusto and relish, so completely "in the midst of things," that has sometimes delighted modern skeptics and atheists who think they see in Ecclesiastes biblical approval for their own empty lives of sensuality and license. But, says Karl Barth:

Ecclesiastes . . . is Epicurean in appearance only: "Go thy way, eat thy bread with a merry heart; for God now accepteth thy works. Let thy garments be always white; and let thy head lack no ointment. Live joyfully with the wife whom thou lovest, all the days of the life of thy vanity, which he hath given thee under the sun. . . . Whatsoever thy hand findeth to do, do it with all thy might; for there is no work, nor device, nor knowl-

edge, nor wisdom, in the grave, whither thou goest." (Eccles. 9:7-10) . . . One surely fails to know the Gospels if he thinks Jesus could not also have said this.[35]

Again, Ecclesiastes knows that "all things are his" to accept and use and enjoy to the fullest. But he knows that "all is his" only as a gift from God, and therefore his only on the basis of his *primary* relationship of obedience to God. This is the very same basis Jesus was talking about when he said, "Seek first [God's] kingdom and his righteousness, and all these things shall be yours as well" (Mt. 6:33). No longer is Ecclesiastes a slave to the things of the world and to the inevitable consequences of such slavery— anxiety, wretchedness, disappointment, boredom, "vanity." Rather, he counsels "sitting loose" in relation to the things of the world. But one cannot "sit loose" in relation to one thing without holding firmly to another. And therefore he tells us, "The best course is never to commit oneself totally to any one thing; for he who fears God will place his complete trust in nothing else" (7:18). Even though the ultimate purposes and plans of God are still hidden from Ecclesiastes' view, he simply takes it for granted that God has revealed enough of himself to Israel to enable his chosen people to *obey*. For it is only in obedience to—or in "the fear of"—God alone that life's greatest "enjoyment" or "pleasure" is given to man here and now. Thus an essential element in the message of Ecclesiastes is also an essential part of the gospel, the "good news," of the New Testament—the "good news, that you should turn from these vain things [or 'vanities'— KJV] to a living God who made the heaven and the earth and . . . did not leave himself without witness . . ." (Acts 14:15, 17).

Pleasure Principle #2—Life's Greatest Pleasure Comes Only from Obedience to God Alone and from No Idol, Not Even Man's First (and Last) Idol—Himself

Man's most *subtle* idol—and therefore the idol

most destructive to man and difficult to root out of his heart—is himself. Even when all of the "things" of the world which men can worship and serve as gods—fame, wisdom, wealth, love, health, power, possessions, sensual pleasure and the rest—even when all of these fail to provide the satisfaction men seek from them, and in this way prove themselves to be "false gods," men can still feel they have their *own* strength, or "inner resources," to fall back on:

> It matters not how strait the gate,
> How charged with punishments the scroll,
> I am the master of my fate;
> I am the captain of my soul.[36]

These lines from the nineteenth-century poem "Invictus" express perfectly man's basic sin of "pride" (or "self-deification"), the basis for *all* of man's disobedience to God.

Ecclesiastes, and the New Testament with him, are quite sure that, as Jesus could say, "No one can serve *two* masters; for either he will hate the one and love the other, or he will be devoted to the one and despise the other" (Mt. 6:24). This means that if *finally* "I am the master of my fate and captain of my soul," then—logically enough—*God* cannot at the same time be my master and my captain. Or, to extend this logic one step further, if I should still insist that *both* God and "I" are my masters, then—because no man can serve *two* masters—God and I would have to be *one*. In other words, *I* would have to be God! But this is just what I've always wanted!

Man has always wanted to be his own god or "master" because after all, if he is confident of anything it is that *he* has his own best interest at heart. Of whom or what else can he say this? But as far as the Bible is concerned, man's self-deification or "pride" or desire to be his own master is man's *basic*—or "origin-al"—sin in two ways: First, it is *the* sin with which all men origin-ate or come into life; men do not begin their lives with a basic trust in God but always begin by trusting primarily in themselves. And, second, it is precisely on the basis of this *sin* that

all of men's *sins* have their *origin*. The poetic story of how this sin came about was fashioned and placed "in the beginning" of the Bible in order to tell us that self-deification is indeed our *basic* sin:

Now the serpent . . . more subtle than any other wild creature that the Lord God had made . . . said to the woman, "You will not die. For God knows that when you eat of the tree your eyes will be opened, and you will be like God, knowing good and evil (Gen. 3:1, 4-5).

Bonhoeffer explicates this crucial passage of Scripture in this way:

Instead of accepting the choice and election of God, man himself desires to choose, to be the origin of the election. . . . Instead of knowing himself solely in the reality of being chosen and loved by God, he must now know himself in the possibility of choosing and of being the origin of good and evil. He has become like God, but against God. Herein lies the serpent's deceit. . . . the good and evil that [man] knows are not the good and evil of God but good and evil against God. They are good and evil of man's own choosing, in opposition to the eternal election of God. In becoming like God man has become a god against God.[37]

To put it another way, man's own choosing, his "free will," is really only a euphemism for man's most subtle form of idolatry—self-deification. If I can *freely* choose good or evil for myself, then I am finally "the master of my own fate." And since one's final "master" is by definition one's god, and a man can have only one master or god, then I must therefore be my own god. In insisting on my own autonomy or "free will," I have actually "become a god against God." Thus it is man's own idolatrous desire to "be like God" that forces him to claim God's free will as his own, to deny his own total finitude and hence to deny that only God is God.

There is no biblical author who lays heavier stress on the fact that man is in no way God, but that only God in heaven is God, than Ecclesiastes. This is why Luther could say, "This book ought really to have the title, 'Against the Free Will.' "[38] "No other writer," says biblical theologian Bernhard Anderson, "puts more emphasis on the sovereignty of God."[39] The term "sovereignty of God" points to the biblical belief that it is God alone who is in charge and in control, who is "sovereign," over absolutely everything that happens—past, present or future. This means that in this view it is also God who causes what men call "evil" and it is God who is behind all of man's feeble little choices or "decisions," including the choices arrogant man arrogates to his own "free will."

That this is Ecclesiastes' view is so apparent that it cannot be obscured by even the worst or most archaic translations available of his book. The famous poem of "the times and seasons" (3:1-9) is a case in point. From the more traditional renderings that there is "a time to kill," "a time to hate," a "time for war," etc., a reader can easily receive the impression that there are indeed times when it is proper for men, in their "freedom," to hate, to kill, to go to war, etc. But it is Ecclesiastes' meaning that the various times and seasons of all life are never dependent upon the "free will" man thinks he has, but are totally dependent upon the truly free will of God. We have therefore said in our translation that there is "a time *of* . . . ," rather than using the traditional "a time to. . . ." For there can be no doubt that this brings us closer to what Ecclesiastes is actually telling us. As R. B. Y. Scott points out:

The various actions named are carried out apparently at man's volition—all but the first. The times of his birth and death are not his to decide, and this gives us the clue to Qoheleth's meaning. Just as surely as birth and death, so all other events and human actions take place when and as God deems them fitting. . . . What happens to man is predetermined by God, and man is in no position to argue with omnipotence.[40]

The very fact that man's smug self-righteousness or "self-deification" or "pride" or "free will" is man's deepest and *final* stronghold against

God, accounts for the completely merciless and unrelenting No! Ecclesiastes hurls at this deadliest of all of man's idols—man himself. His book is largely a remorseless polemic against the pride of man in general, but also against the way in which this pride had become a virtual *doctrine* of Israel's "wisdom schools" in particular. This school of thought is best represented in the Old Testament by the friends of Job, who were quite sure that Job had "freely" brought all of his troubles on himself and that all he needed to do to correct things was "freely" to pull himself up by his own spiritual bootstraps. But Job—and especially Ecclesiastes—know this is not the way life operates. Ecclesiastes was at odds with the wisdom of the schools because he saw them as being supremely overoptimistic about man's own abilities and this at God's expense. The "wise man" at whom Ecclesiastes is sniping not only claims to be able to "unscrew the inscrutable" and fathom the unfathomable mysteries of God; this unwise "wise man" also claims to *have control* over God. Such is the case with all men of "free will." They themselves become the "prime mover," God being only the helpless re-actor to the action men themselves initiate. Theologian Walther Zimmerli puts it this way:

Ecclesiastes is the frontier-guard, who forbids Wisdom to cross the frontier towards a comprehensive art of life. He secures the right interpretation of the sentence: "The fear of the Lord is the beginning of knowledge". . . . He who fears God knows that God is the Lord, and that, if it is God's will, even the highest human Wisdom can break down and become deep foolishness. The fear of God never allows man in his "art of directing" to hold the helm in his own hands. Wisdom . . . is possible when it is willing to seize only the portion and not the whole—when it is willing to enjoy the gift that God gives today and will not try to make God's promise an item in the calculation of man's life. The fear of God remains open to God Himself— the free and living God. Hence Ecclesiastes reminds Wisdom of its place before the creator.[44]

Ecclesiastes was a "wise man" himself, but a

86

"chastened" wise man. That is, his conclusions about man's inability to save himself through either his own wisdom or his own actions were learned the hard way—by going all the way down these dead-end streets himself, the same way he learned of the "vanity" behind all of the vanities he tested. In Ecclesiastes' "attempt to master the world 'by wisdom,' which means 'by knowledge and active life,' he encounters the reality of the creator more clearly than any other Israelite wise man before him. Everywhere he meets with a reality that is determined and cannot be apprehended. Behind all this determination and all this ability not to be apprehended it is God, who cannot be scrutinised, who is free, who never reacts, but always acts in freedom" (Zimmerli).[42]

In this struggle of one man, Ecclesiastes, against the proud self-idolization of the men of the wisdom schools, it is possible to see a rehearsal of remarkable likeness to the struggles that took place later when Jesus opposed the Pharisees, when St. Paul opposed the "Judaizing" elements in the early church, and when Luther opposed the medieval church. Common to all of these conflicts was the one question: Who *finally* is man's master? Man himself or God? But what is even more remarkable is the way in which this same struggle takes shape today. As we have seen, it was belief in God's deity that first freed man from the enslaving "powers" of the world and thus enabled man to put nature to work for him. But once this process of "secularization" has been set in motion by faith, it can continue without faith. When this happens, man becomes completely alone in the universe—no gods, no God, only himself lost in the utter darkness of the surrounding void. Modern scientific man knows that he is completely a pawn of nature; he knows that even in his "own" controlling, all of his smallest actions are themselves finally controlled by blind, impersonal "laws of nature." In this thoroughgoing "determinism" modern man and Ecclesiastes are very much in agreement. Both can

actually see, with their own eyes, that they are not in control of their own destinies, but rather that they themselves are controlled by forces other than themselves. But whereas Ecclesiastes, on the basis of his heart, believes that God is that "Other" behind the "predestination" of the world, modern man—totally dependent on his eyes and thus having lost all heart—sees nothing but the indifferent clockwork of nature. Hence modern man is thrown completely back on himself to find any meaning in life. If man's existence is to have any meaning at all, man himself must now create this meaning. And thus modern man is trapped in a paradoxical situation: while he correctly sees that he is only a tiny, finite part of nature, at the same time he is forced to believe the lie that he himself is "the Creator." For as Camus could clearly see, "To kill God is to become God oneself."[43]

But modern man can live only on one side of this paradox or the other, although he truly believes both sides to be true. Naturally his first inclination is to think the best of himself, and so he sees himself as his own meaning-giver. On the basis of one alien ideology (or "wisdom") after another, modern man himself becomes the world's savior in his "autonomous" attempts to perfect the world by giving it unity and coherence. The result is not man's liberation as was hoped, but only the increase of his servitude. For man, who is imperfect, is made the slave of an alien system of perfection.

The "dethroning of all autonomous wisdom is also the concern of Koheleth, when he indeed acknowledges wisdom within its limits as a high good, but at the same time throws a fierce light on its 'vanity' so far as ultimate questions are concerned, by his profound meditations on the power of God in creation" (Eichrodt). Because of its purity and remoteness from faith, it is *science* which today best personifies man's "autonomous" or self-proud wisdom. And therefore just as Ecclesiastes could act as a stubborn, "frontier-guard" against the presumptuous wisdom of his own time, as Zimmerli pointed out, so the "wise men" of today are still pointedly confronted by Koheleth's sharp and unyielding No! For it is indeed true that Ecclesiastes is out to dethrone *all* autonomous wisdom, and that means

to draw the boundary between the areas where scientific method is appropriate and where it is not, that is, to pronounce the "vanity of vanities" on human endeavor. This is possibly the most useful function that Koheleth's words could discharge in our times. Amid the confusions of what is now universally called a "scientific age," the astringent "vanity of vanities" is urgently required that men may know where and where not the application of scientific technique and judgment is appropriate. Koheleth sets the limits. No science may provide a man with that which is ultimately profitable and worth-while, or with that which provides final satisfaction and meaning. Science may press out to the boundaries, but beyond there is a larger value, a fuller worth, and a dimension of experience, which are just not amenable to scientific investigation. . . . Scientific inquiry is concerned with matter of fact and not the determination of value, or profit, as Ecclesiastes would have said. Civilisation will be eclipsed if technical capacity is pursued for its own sake, as an end in itself. . . . Still more will civilisation be eclipsed, should the methods of science, because of the prestige which their success in their proper fields has brought them, ever come to be applied in areas of life where they are inappropriate. (Johnstone)[44]

This "eclipse of civilization," which even now is in the process of occurring, is the result of the constant meaninglessness to which modern man is exposed in his attempt to "go it alone"—the attempt to rely finally on his own wisdom for providing the world with ultimate meaning. And hence the collapse of this side of the paradox that modern man holds to be true, the side that insists that he must be his own meaning-giver, forces him to live on the paradox's other side, the side that says that there is no God and that man is only an animal. And when man thinks of himself as "only an animal," he will begin acting like an animal. This is the deterioration of

modern man's presumptuous wisdom into the chaos and despair of *nihilism*, and is the very same deterioration St. Paul was describing when he wrote:

Claiming to be wise, they became fools. . . . Therefore God gave them up in the lusts of their hearts to impurity, to the dishonoring of their bodies among themselves, because they exchanged the truth about God for a lie and worshiped and served the creature rather than the Creator. . . . Since they did not see fit to acknowledge God, God gave them up to a base mind and to improper conduct. (Rom. 1:21-22, 25, 28)

Ecclesiastes never uses the word "nihilism," but he has a word of his own for it—"bestiality." Indeed Ecclesiastes has himself often been accused of being a nihilist precisely because he sees *man in and of himself* as being a totally finite animal:

For man is controlled by fate exactly as animals are controlled by fate; and one final fate awaits them both—death! They both draw the same breath of life; and man's advantage over other beasts is nothing, for all is a breath that vanishes. (3:19)

But "Ecclesiastes is anything but a nihilistic agnostic" (von Rad).[45] For he knows that man is that creature of God with whom God has created a special relationship: man can "acknowledge God," to use St. Paul's phrase. And thus for Ecclesiastes as well as for Paul it is only this very acknowledgment that can save men not only from the enslaving myth that their own "infinite" wisdom can supply them with meaning, but also from the "bestial behavior" caused by this proud belief's inevitable fall into nihilism:

In this wicked behavior of men, I reflected, God is limiting them in order to show them their own finitude and their bestial behavior to each other. (3:18)

According to Bonhoeffer, "nihilism" is the underlying characteristic of modern man.[46] No doubt this is true. There is also no doubt that Ecclesiastes, being so intimately acquainted with the "ins and outs" of nihilism, can give us great insight not only into how modern man got in this situation, but also how he can find a way out.

But modern man is also *religious,* is he not? Indeed he can be. But the fact is that the more basic cultural religion of "Man the Self-Sufficient" so permeates the life of modern man that even his so-called "worship of God"—as well as his "theology"!—is deeply infected with it. Modern man's "religiosity" is largely just that —a thin religious veneer behind which he still trusts primarily in himself as "the master of his own fate, the captain of his own soul." Ecclesiastes reserves his strongest terms for those who mask an ultimate trust in themselves, their *own* ability to win God's favor, behind an outward show of piety. He calls them "fools" (5:1). The poster in the picture I have used to illustrate this verse is a perfect contemporary expression of the "religious" self-righteousness so abhorrent to Ecclesiastes. Like St. Paul, Ecclesiastes is unrelenting in his attack at this point because he sees clearly that the "religious" man is fundamentally different from no one else: The very last thing *anyone* wants to relinquish before God is the idol of one's *own* "free will," one's *own* righteousness, one's *own* control of one's own destiny. The "religious" man is just a bit *shrewder* in his attempts to remain his own master: "What I am may be God's gift to me . . . but what *I make of myself* is my free and big-hearted gift to God. Therefore God *is in debt to me.*" Naturally this point of view, which gives men control over God, will always be more popular than the biblical attitude on the subject, namely: "Who could ever give God anything or lend him anything? *All* that exists comes from him; *all* is by him and for him" (Rom. 11:35, 36 *The Jerusalem Bible*).

And yet, even though Ecclesiastes would thoroughly agree with Jesus that "No one is good but God alone" (Mk. 10:18; cf. Eccles. 7:20), like Jesus, Ecclesiastes can then turn right around and tell us in the strongest terms to "shape up," just as though we were all freely capable of "doing good" ourselves. For it is obvious that Ecclesiastes was an advocate "of a *positive involvement and participation in life.* We find in this book a resolute opposition to any suggestion of quietism" (Edgar Jones).[47] How then can we reconcile these two seemingly contradictory demands, the demands to *live as though it all depends on you, but believe that it all depends on God?*

Ecclesiastes himself shows us the way. His answer is given to us in a single demand that is constantly repeated throughout the Bible, the demand that we "fear God." For Ecclesiastes, as well as for the rest of the Bible, "the fear of God" is a single power cell with both positive and negative poles. Positively, it means to *obey only God.* For Ecclesiastes "the conclusion of the whole matter" is to "Fear God and obey his commandments! For this is the whole duty of man" (12:13). Negatively, to "fear God" means to expect "trouble" if we do *not* so obey. "He who obeys the command will avoid trouble; for the wise man knows there will be a time of judgment" (8:5). ("Trouble" and "judgment" are to be understood here as occurring *within* a man's lifetime. Ecclesiastes, remember, is not at all sure what—if anything—lies on the other side of death.)

On the basis of this understanding of what it means to "fear God," we can now see that the biblical ax is laid to the root of all human pride or boasting or self-righteousness adhering to men's obedience to God. This happens in three ways: First, the *heart's* way: the *fear* of God alone. Obedience to God is brought about not by our own free wills, but in a way that "leaves us no choice" (2 Cor. 5:14 NEB). We *must* obey God if our hearts are to "avoid trouble"; and if we *must,* there is no place for pride in our own wills. "It is a *fearful* thing to fall into the hands of the living God" (Heb. 10:31). For God meets us not as a harmless beggar, but rather in the same way that men are confronted by "the Godfather": he makes us an offer we cannot refuse! This is exactly why St. Paul, an incorrigible old rebel exactly like the rest of us, could finally say, "Knowing the fear of the Lord, we persuade men" (2 Cor. 5:11). "Even if I preach the Gospel," he says, "I can claim no credit for it; I cannot help myself; it would be *misery* for me not to preach. . . . I do it apart from my own choice . . ." (1 Cor. 9:16, 17 NEB). When President John F. Kennedy was asked how he became a hero in the Second World War, he replied, "It was involuntary. They sank my boat."[48] This is also the precise way in which one *always* becomes a man of faith. For it is not without first going through the harrowing, *involuntary experience* of having the original, false foundation of one's life unceremoniously demolished, that one can then cling to God alone as one's foundation. This is why Norman Snaith can say:

The less a man knows in his own experience of the saving work of God, the more he emphasizes the human element; the more he knows of the grace of God, the more he speaks of it as being decisive in his own life.[49]

Second, the way of the *head*: the fear of God *alone*. For if we are to obey *only* God, which means also to *trust* only in him, then we can understand quite logically that in trusting finally in our own righteousness, or even in our own *abilities* to be righteous, we have thereby failed to trust only in God, to "Seek first [God's] kingdom and *his* righteousness" (Mt. 6:33). Third, the way of the *eyes*: the fear of *God* alone. Our eyes tell us that the modern scientist is correct—that whatever "power" or "powers" are finally in charge of the universe, they are in charge of *all* of it and not just a limited part of it. These forces work with a *visible* constancy and orderliness and universality that for these reasons we can trace and use and depend on every day of our lives. Ecclesiastes *believed* this final "universal Power" was the living God, who just because he was God was completely in control of all things. But in this faith he found confirmation from his own eyes. And thus obedi-

ence only to God meant obedience to the sovereign Power behind the universe, rather than obedience to some helpless, second-rate mini-god, who was simply forced to do the best he could in view of a mysterious phantom called man's "free will." "This I saw and clearly understood," says Ecclesiastes, "that the righteous and the wise and all that they do are controlled by God's hand. . . . All things come to all men from a source beyond their control, just as the same fate can come to any two men . . ." (9:1-2).

For these reasons, then, we can understand how another old rebel, Ecclesiastes, was able to avoid the "obedience" which is undermined by pride in itself, and instead hold fast to the pleasure principle of truly *humble* obedience: "Live as though it all depends on you, but believe that it all depends on God."

E. WHO WAS ECCLESIASTES?

We have saved all questions surrounding the authorship of Ecclesiastes until this point because, after all, *he* was not overly concerned with these questions, so why should we be? But it is true that as soon as we become the least bit familiar with this man's "tiny masterpiece," our curiosities are inevitably pricked to want to know more about him personally.

1. *The Name "Ecclesiastes"*

Since even the very name "Ecclesiastes" tends to be a mouthful, we will try to simplify further matters as much as possible by saying: "Koheleth" is his Hebrew name; "Ecclesiastes" is his Greek name; and "the Preacher" is the name Martin Luther gave him. The Hebrew word "Koheleth" (the "K" is sometimes seen as a "Q" or "C" or even "Ch") is not actually a man's name but a word indicating the *function* of "one who speaks in an assembly or congregation." Since the Greek word for assembly or congregation is *ekklesia* (which is also the Greek word for "church"), the Greek translators of the Bible used the obscure Greek word "Ecclesiastes" to designate such a speaker. Luther figured that because we were dealing with one who spoke to a congregation, the ancient word "Koheleth" should be updated to "the Preacher." But as many commentators have observed, this man was no ordinary preacher!

2. Was Ecclesiastes Solomon?

Up until the sixteenth century, the book of Ecclesiastes was attributed to Solomon and usually thought of as the testament of Solomon in his old age. But since that time biblical scholarship is virtually unanimous in saying that Solomon could not have been the author. This conclusion is largely based on the fact that the language and world-outlook of Ecclesiastes are much more "modern"—by about seven centuries!—than those of Solomon's time. One look at *The Catcher in the Rye* and we know that Shakespeare did not write it. Biblical scholars are able to look at Ecclesiastes and say the same thing about Solomon being its author.

But this raises the intriguing question of why the book's author assumes the role of Solomon, for it is clear from such verses as 1:12-13, 16 and 2:1-9 that he does so. The book's very first verse reads, "The words of Ecclesiastes, David's son, king in Jerusalem"—that is, Solomon. In using this literary fiction, it would seem Ecclesiastes wanted to give his work two types of authority that could be derived from the majestic name of Solomon. First, with Solomon as his authority he can prove one of his major theological theses with dramatic clarity. According to Robert Gordis, Ecclesiastes at the beginning of his book

is seeking to demonstrate that even the ultimate of wisdom and luxury possible to man has no absolute value or significance. What more effective device than to have this view of the vanity of life expressed by Solomon, who symbolized both these goals of human striving? Any lesser figure might be charged with being an incompetent witness. . . .

This purpose accomplished, the role of Solomon is laid aside for the remaining five-sixths of the book, never to be resumed.[50]

But Ecclesiastes also wants to claim, in opposition to the wisdom schools, that he stands in the *true* tradition of the wisdom of Solomon and David. According to Gordis, Ecclesiastes "makes no effort to imply seriously that Solomon is the author."[51] Why, asks Gordis, if Ecclesiastes had really intended "to palm his work off as the work of Solomon," did he not expressly use the name "Solomon" rather than the enigmatic name "Koheleth"? Part of the answer to this question must be that although it was known to Ecclesiastes' immediate contemporaries that he was certainly not Solomon, Ecclesiastes nevertheless wanted to claim that the wisdom he represented—rather than the wisdom of the schools—was the genuine article and stood squarely in the venerable tradition of Solomon's own wisdom. This personation was a literary device commonly used in Ecclesiastes' time and, as *The New American Bible* puts it, is a device intended "to lend greater dignity and authority to the book—a circumstance which does not in any way impugn its inspired character."[52] At the same time, Jacques Ellul is no doubt right in saying that tradition itself shows great wisdom in placing "Ecclesiastes under the name of Solomon. It is precisely the wise man who knows that he is not wise, and that unless God gives him the knowledge of the good in his revelation, he knows nothing and is living in folly."[53]

3. Was Ecclesiastes Written by One Man or Nine?

During the heyday of nineteenth-century biblical "higher criticism" it was the fashion to tear apart the various books of the Bible by seeing in each of them the contributions of sometimes many different authors. Although there was a certain amount of validity to some of this scholarly investigation, this was also the kind of academic enterprise that could reach the point of absurdity in a hurry. Ecclesiastes did not escape being pulled apart in this way. At one point the book was seen as the compiled work of as many as nine authors[54]—a conclusion which itself verifies Ecclesiastes' warnings about the close relationship between folly and wisdom!

Today, however, scholars are inclined to see the book as "a literary unit, the spiritual testament of a single, complex, richly endowed personality" (Gordis).[55] A few scholars still see odd bits of tinkering here and there; but generally, as the editors of *The Jerusalem Bible* tell us, "there is a growing dislike for any dissection that betrays a misunderstanding of the book's literary form and of its theme."[56] But it must also be admitted that Ecclesiastes was an attractive candidate for being hacked to pieces by the scholarly imagination. For many of the things he says do seem to be contradictory *on the basis of appearances alone*. We emphasize the latter because it is only on the basis of mere appearances that Ecclesiastes could be understood as anything other than a literary whole. This is why some of the recent fiascos of biblical criticism carry with them the important lesson that the Bible must be read with the *heart* as well as with the *head*. This rule is certainly nowhere truer than it is in the case of Ecclesiastes. "Koheleth can be comprehended only if approached with sympathy and insight," says Gordis.[57] This means that if we have understood Ecclesiastes on the level that it was meant to be understood, on the level of "sympathy and insight," if we let the book speak for itself and do not impose our own preconceived ideas on it, there is absolutely no necessity to think that *any* part of it was written by anyone other than a single man. The author of Ecclesiastes was a complex individual, just as we would expect any sensitive person to be who lived "between the times" as he did. And therefore "rather than explain the self-corrections and self-contradictions by a plurality of authors, it would seem preferable to attribute them to the oscillation of one man's mind confronted with a

mystery of mysteries and lacking the data for a solution" (*The Jerusalem Bible*).[58] This is why it is always best to think of "Ecclesiastes" as a *man's name*, rather than the *title* of a lifeless thing. For in dealing with Ecclesiastes we are confronted with all of the unpredictable complexity, and yet unifying integrity and wholeness, of a living individual.[59]

F. SO, THEN, WHO WAS ECCLESIASTES REALLY?

Ecclesiastes was an upper-class teacher of wisdom who lived in Jerusalem about three centuries before Christ. Beyond this there is little more about the man that we need to know—or indeed *can* know—in order to appreciate his book. As we have seen, appreciation and sympathy for Ecclesiastes is a feat that comes with unwelcome ease for us moderns. In the meantime, recent theological inquiry has been exerting great efforts in tracking down Modern Man, Secular Man, Man Come of Age—trying to learn just who this beast is and what he looks like. It is telling and ironic that theology has gone so far afield in looking for the answer to this question when all the while there stands the very prototype of Modern Man in—of all places!—the Bible. For the questions and doubts of Ecclesiastes are easily identified as our questions and doubts; his method of seeking an answer is our method; and his despair has led him down the same blind alleys in which we have so often lost our ways. Therefore we of today are fortunate to have in the Bible such an eloquent and forceful spokesman for our ways of looking at things: today we are skeptics and sophisticates and relentless seekers for the truth. But compared with Ecclesiastes we are all amateurs in these pursuits—he has "outskepticked" and outsophisticated and outsought the best of us. For these and more reasons Ecclesiastes is for us today the truest of all the Bible's books. And hence the truth in Atkins' statement: "No book in the Bible reflects more sensitively, allowing for all the differences, the moods and phases of our always deeply shadowed time."[60]

It is also highly significant that Ecclesiastes was one of the last, if not *the* last book of the Hebrew Bible written before the time of Christ. This fact is especially important when we remember that Ecclesiastes remains radically "open-ended" in his view of things. He understands *the answers* that he finally comes up with as only several pieces to the greater puzzle of *the Answer*. If the question of modern man is "What do I do until the undertaker comes?" Ecclesiastes' question is even more uncertain: "What do I do until the Messiah comes?—*if* he comes!" In the final analysis, "Ecclesiastes endeavors to stand although he is broken down" (Zimmerli);[61] ". . . nothing remained for Ecclesiastes but to submit in deep resignation to this tragic existence" (von Rad).[62] Thus his testimony ends more with a whimper than a bang; more with a question mark than an exclamation point.

The deeply searching questions Ecclesiastes leaves us with point clearly in the direction of the answer of the New Testament. But we must never move into this area too quickly. We ourselves must first have really heard—and felt—the extremely hard questions that Ecclesiastes puts to us—questions put to us simply on the basis of an honest, tough-minded look at life itself. The major difficulty with most decidedly "Christian interpretations" of Ecclesiastes has been that they have not taken seriously enough the fact that his book does end with a whimper and not with a bang. They have been too anxious to see Christ in Ecclesiastes without first facing up to the "fine hammered steel of woe" of the book's final resolution. Or, as Melville ends his famous description of Ecclesiastes: " 'All is vanity.' ALL. This wilful world hath not got hold of unchristian Solomon's wisdom yet."[63] And this is precisely why Bonhoeffer could write from his prison cell:

My thoughts and feelings seem to be getting more and more like those of the Old Testament, and in recent months I have been reading the Old Testament much more than the New. . . . In my opinion it is not Christian to want to take our thoughts and feelings too quickly and too directly from the New Testament. . . . One cannot and must not speak the last word before the last but one.[64]

It is that "last but one word" that Ecclesiastes sums up and speaks so forcefully to us. But having now seen and read and pondered that word, it is to "the last word" that we turn next.

III

Ecclesiastes: The Bible's Negative Image of Christ the Truth

I, Ecclesiastes, was king over Israel in Jerusalem.

—Ecclesiastes 1:12

Turning to his disciples in private Jesus said, "Happy the eyes that see what you are seeing! I tell you, many prophets and kings wished to see what you now see, yet never saw it; to hear what you hear, yet never heard it."

—Luke 10:23, 24 NEB

All these persons died in faith. They were not yet in possession of the things promised, but had seen them far ahead and hailed them, and confessed themselves no more than strangers or passing travellers on earth.

—Hebrews 11:13, NEB

One must . . . really speak of a witness of the Old Testament to Christ, for our knowledge of Christ is incomplete without the witness of the Old Testament. Christ is given to us only through the double witness of the choir of those who await and those who remember.

—Gerhard von Rad[1]

Ecclesiastes is the most moving Messianic prophecy in the Old Testament.

—H. W. Hertzberg[2]

Ecclesiastes seems to me to be the book of hope above all others.

—Jacques Ellul, *Hope in Time of Abandonment*, 1973[3]

1. Ecclesiastes: The Bible's Most Powerfully Concentrated Expression of What Christ Is

"The Old Testament tells us *what* the Christ is; the New *who* he is." This statement by Wilhelm Vischer is hard to improve as a succinct summary of the relationship between the two Testaments. For, continues Vischer,

Christianity means precisely the confession that Jesus is the Christ in the sense in which the Old Testament defines Israel's Messiah. . . . It is not the case that we know what the designation "Christ" means. When the New Testament declares that Jesus is the Christ it immediately refers us to the Old: Learn there what Christ means. With this in mind the primitive Church retained the Old Testament as sacred scripture.[4]

And, as Vischer also points out, the Old Testament writings alone were "*the* Scriptures" for the first Christians. As St. Paul could say of the Old Testament, "whatever was written in former days was written for our instruction, that by steadfastness and by encouragement of the scriptures we might have hope" (Rom. 15:4).

The church has always held that the Old and New Testaments must interpret each other. The classic rule has been: the New Testament is *concealed* within the Old—the Old Testament is *revealed* by the New. "What is patent in the New Testament is latent in the Old" is another way of expressing this famous saying by St. Augustine. This means, first of all, that from the New Testament perspective there is absolutely no way of understanding the Old Testament as it was meant to be understood apart from the "clue" of Christ. Thus Christ is described by the disciples as the one who "opened to us the scrip-

tures" (Lk. 24:32). "You search the scriptures," said Jesus, "because you think that in them you have eternal life; and it is they that bear witness to me" (Jn. 5:39). But on the other hand, it is also true that the New Testament insists that there is absolutely no way of understanding Christ as *he* was meant to be understood apart from the Old Testament. "The strongest resistance to any idea of abandoning the Old Testament comes from the New Testament itself," says biblical theologian Gerhard von Rad. "For its testimony to Christ can only be divorced from its Old Testament background at the cost of very radical reinterpretation."[5] When Christ came into the world, he did not come into some kind of vague "never-never land." He specifically "came to his own" (Jn. 1:11); and the New Testament goes to great pains to demonstrate that this "his own" is far from being a matter of indifference. For not unless the church first understands this "his own"—that is, the story of the people of the Old Testament—can it then really understand why Christ came in the first place. To attempt to understand the New Testament without its Old Testament background is like trying to understand a specific *answer* without first understanding "its own" specific *question* to which this answer is addressed. "For Jesus is the fulfillment of the Old Testament promises. The fulfiller is inseparable from that of which he is the fulfillment" (Braaten).[6] Or, to return to Vischer's way of putting it, if Christians were to abandon the Old Testament, they would no longer know *what* the Christ is. As far as the New Testament is concerned, *Jesus is the Christ of the Old Testament.*

With what we have just said in mind, let us now state the following thesis as clearly as possible: *Ecclesiastes is the Bible's most powerfully concentrated expression of* what *Christ is.* It would almost appear that for some time biblical scholarship has been approaching this conclusion. For whereas one biblical scholar will see Ecclesiastes to be absolutely unique in one way, another scholar will see his uniqueness to lie elsewhere: Ecclesiastes is "the "quintessence of scepticism" (Heine);[7] "the quintessence of piety" (Delitzsch);[8] "Koheleth, as none before him, completes the de-personalization of the natural order" (Eichrodt);[9] Ecclesiastes "encounters the reality of the creator more clearly than any other Israelite wise man before him" (Zimmerli);[10] "Only with the Book of Ecclesiastes did [Israel's] scepticism emerge . . . with an unheard of radicality and weight" (von Rad);[11] "No other writer puts more emphasis on the sovereignty of God" (Anderson).[12] As more and more of many such superlative stands of opinion on Ecclesiastes are pulled together, it becomes clear that this deceptively brief book is a uniquely concentrated expression of the Old Testament itself, and therefore is the Bible's most powerfully concentrated expression of *what* Christ is.

It is no accident that such an intensification of Israel's self-expression occurs when it does—just at the close of that period when her Bible was written. Von Rad, "widely recognized as the world's most important Old Testament theologian,"[13] tells us "that the Old Testament can only be read as a book in which expectation keeps mounting up to vast proportions." The Old Testament, he says, is "a book of ever increasing anticipation, . . . of ever more powerfully concentrated expectation. . . . This forward-looking is certainly not always the same. Sometimes it is more obvious, sometimes less: but it is present everywhere. . . ."[14] Why does this heightening of anticipation and expectation occur? Paradoxical as it may sound, Israel's anticipation of God increases in direct relation to the way in which God becomes more and more hidden from her. The more Israel's God hides himself from her, the more eagerly he is sought and hoped for. "The whole history of the covenant is simply the history of God's continuous retreat," says von Rad. Israel's God is the God who "hides himself ever more deeply from his people, who kills Israel in order to bring her to life again."[15] It is the way of the father who withdraws from his child for a while in order that the child may be taught to trust *only* in the father, rather than trusting in the father's many gifts to the child. Faith is belief in God *alone,* and therefore it has no props or proofs other than its own inner conviction. And thus when God brings a man to stand alone before him as a mature man of faith, God will first hide himself from that man. For when God is hidden, only *faith* in him will then suffice; props and proofs will be of no avail. "The supreme analogy between the Old and New Testaments," says von Rad, "is the way in which men are confronted more and more painfully with a God who continually retreats from them, and [in face of] whom they have only the gamble of faith to rest on."[16]

2. *Ecclesiastes: A Christ-Shaped Vacuum*

This brings us to the second part of our thesis: Ecclesiastes, as the Bible's most powerfully concentrated expression of *what* Christ is, *is a "Christ-shaped vacuum."* Israel had known many "vacuums" during the long history of her dealings with God. "In one way or another," says von Rad, ". . . Israel was always placed in the vacuum between an election made manifest in her history, and which had a definite promise attached to it, and a fulfillment of this promise which was looked for in the future."[17] We wish to contend, however, that precisely here, in the "vanity of vanities" of Ecclesiastes, we come face to face with *the* vacuum of all of Israel's many vacuums. When Christ came into the world, he came as "the light [that] shines in the *darkness*" (Jn. 1:5, 9). And precisely here, in Ecclesiastes, we have the clearest expression of *the* darkness, *the* vacuum, into which Christ came as *the* light and *the* fulfillment. As "a Christ-shaped vacuum," then, Ecclesiastes has three important aspects that should be spelled out.

a. No vacuum can exist without a strong enclosure. The stronger the vacuum, the stronger its enclosure must be for the vacuum to remain a vacuum. Just because "nature abhors a vacuum," any vacuum will vanish as soon as its enclosure collapses. The enclosure surrounding the vacuum of Ecclesiastes is strong indeed—it is no less than God himself. It is *God* who has bracketed Ecclesiastes' life with questions "from the beginning to the end" (3:11). And Ecclesiastes knows this, as Johannes Hempel makes clear:

He is not a sceptic from disbelief, but he belongs to the circles of genuine Israelite piety for which the otherness of God is a central element of religious experience. In this he takes refuge, and on this footing he wrestles for a solution to the perplexity of life, for an answer to the question why the course of life seems aimless and meaningless. Just because God is God, the true nature of His creation and of His activity cannot be grasped. . . .[18]

So great is the intensity with which Ecclesiastes questions God, that what he and Israel *already* know of God is refined to its absolute essence. St. Paul neatly expresses this essence—the essence of what could "be known about God" in pre-Christian times—as "his invisible nature, namely his eternal power and deity" (Rom. 1:19-20). (Generally speaking, in Part II we were discussing Ecclesiastes' knowledge of God's *power* under "Pleasure Principle #2" and God's *deity* under "Pleasure Principle # 1.") This distillation of the Old Testament's knowledge of God is in no way superseded or nullified by God's further self-revelation in Christ. Christ did not come to destroy the "laws" of God's power and deity, but to fulfill them by giving them aim and meaning. What Ecclesiastes knows with utter clarity about God, the New Testament likewise knows and is in full agreement. This then is their common knowledge of God that provides a *positive* link between the two Testaments.

b. It is the nature of a vacuum to seek its own fulfillment, and the same is true of the vacuum of Ecclesiastes. Says von Rad, "This tragedy is the book's theme—in this world devoid of all action of [God] in history, Ecclesiastes seeks for God."[19] It is not true that Ecclesiastes has given up all hope of finding an answer to the question of life's meaning. He knows as well as anyone that "Where there's life, there's hope." Or, as he puts it, "Only the living have any hope; and therefore a living dog is better than a dead lion" (9:4). Job, Ecclesiastes' predecessor in confronting God with brutal frankness, tried to wrest an answer from God almost by sheer force; but Job is now a dead lion. All that is left for Ecclesiastes is to whimper before God like a dog; but he does have hope. And like the Canaanite woman who begged like a dog at the feet of Jesus (Mt. 15; Mk. 7), it is the very hopelessness of Ecclesiastes' hope that brings him so near to the New Testament's fulfillment of that hope. This is why Bonhoeffer's earlier statement is again so apropos: "The world that has come of age is more godless, and perhaps for that very reason nearer to God, than the world before its coming of age." For whether we are considering the radical "godlessness" of modern man or the utter skepticism of Ecclesiastes, both forms of doubt only represent the process of "making room for God"—that painful purgation of all props, proofs and "false gods" which must take place in men's hearts before God himself will claim his rightful place there. The completely vacuous hearts of the godless and the honest skeptic alike are therefore one step "nearer to God" than those hearts which are filled only with an idol as God.

"To an increasing degree," says von Rad, Israel's

later period spoke of the impossibility of knowing Jahweh [God]. To know Jahweh was previously the glory and privilege of Israel. But alongside this idea deriving from the distant past—it was not removed—there are more and more references to the incomprehensibility of Jahweh. . . . However, only with the Book of Ecclesiastes did this scepticism emerge broadly based and with a hitherto unheard of radicality and weight.[20]

Thus it is clear that Ecclesiastes represents the final stage of the Old Testament's preparation for the coming of Christ. Israel has in no way forgotten what she has already learned of God. But in Ecclesiastes this knowledge of God's power and deity is now reduced to its most concentrated form and is accompanied by a similarly purified expression for what Israel *still* wants to know of God. All aspects of Old Testament thought converge like lines on a cone pointing toward the single point of Jesus the Messiah. But the last tiny portion of the tip of that cone, through which all of the lines must pass and are therefore necessarily concentrated and simplified, is Ecclesiastes, the Hebrew Bible's single final link to Christ. "Christ Jesus of the New Testament stands precisely at the vanishing point of Old Testament perspective," says Vischer;[21] and Ecclesiastes is precisely that "vanishing point." Nowhere is the Old Testament as "old" as it is in this one book which forms the doorway to the New. "Words cannot describe the weariness of all things," he tells us (1:8). And therefore it is not surprising that the basic forms taken by the New Testament's *answers* find their closest opposite numbers in Ecclesiastes' *questions*:

Ecclesiastes: "There is nothing new under the sun" (1:9).
New Testament: "A new commandment I give to you" (Jn. 13:34); "Therefore, if anyone is in Christ, he is a new creation; the old has passed away, behold, the new has come" (2 Cor. 5:17); "Behold, I make all things new" (Rev. 21:5).
Ecclesiastes: "Emptiness, emptiness, says the Speaker, emptiness, all is empty" (1:2; 12:8 NEB).
New Testament: "When the fulness of time was come, God sent forth his son" (Gal. 4:4 KJV); "And [Jesus] began to say to them, 'Today this scripture has been fulfilled in your hearing'" (Lk. 4:21).

And thus Ecclesiastes is essentially a kind of negative theologian, asking questions that can be answered only by a future revelation of God, and clearing the road for this revelation by smashing any and all false hopes to pieces. He represents that vacuum of vacuums in Israel's history when her knowledge of God was felt to be grievously inadequate and yet nothing new had come forth to complete this knowledge. "By underlining the inadequacies of earlier notions and by compelling reconsideration of the human enigma," says *The Jerusalem Bible*, Ecclesiastes "exposes the need of a new revelation."[22] Ecclesiastes is the Bible's "night before Christmas."

c. As a "Christ-shaped" vacuum, Ecclesiastes anticipates the actual "form" that will be taken by the coming Christ. Here again Ecclesiastes is like a photographer. For it is only by first creating a *negative* image that a photographer—one who "writes with light"—can then produce a positive or "true" picture. A photographer uses an initial source of light to take his picture and to produce a "negative." Then, in his darkroom, this negative is placed against light-sensitive paper. At this point another burst of light is needed, a light strong enough to pass through the negative, casting the negative's shadows onto the paper. And in this way a positive picture is formed as an exact counterpart of a negative image. This is also what we see happening between the two Testaments. "These," says the New Testament of the events taking place in the Old, "are only a shadow of what is to come; but the substance belongs to Christ" (Col. 2:17). Ecclesiastes especially is "an exact negative counterpart" to the form and substance of Christ. In Ecclesiastes, the following statement by von Rad finds its truest expression:

It has been said that all that the [biblical] narrators described . . . is narrated with reference to the future. One must only add the further point that this future is in no sense a vague one, hidden, let us say, in the counsel of God, but a definite, and therefore known future. And this we term a "fulfillment," the content of which is exactly determined by an antecedent promise.[23]

This does not mean that the New Testament figure of Jesus is cut to fit the pattern of the Old. "That it pleased God at that time and place and in that way to reveal Himself in the name of Jesus Christ, is something which had its necessity in itself, and not in circumstances and conditions prior to that name" (Barth).[24] Old Testament prophecy is not laid down as a plan that God must follow. As far as the Old Testament is concerned, prophecy is true prophecy only if God has already chosen to fulfill it and therefore has himself sent his prophet as precursor of the future (cf. Jer. 28:9). Nevertheless, when he sends a prophet into the world, God, like the wise actor described by Shakespeare, "suits the action to the word, the word to the action."[25] And as it happens, the once-and-for-all questions raised by Ecclesiastes are perfectly suited to the once-and-for-all answer of God's Word, Jesus Christ. The New Testament is the "good news" of the One who came to fulfill the deepest of all human needs. And Ecclesiastes, as the Bible's clearest expression for what that need is, is *prophetic*—in the positive or "foretelling" sense of prophecy—in giving us an exact outline of *what* this "fulfiller" will be. Ecclesiastes is human self-sufficiency stretched to its absolute limit and found sadly wanting. But if we look closely at exactly what this "want" is, we can see clearly that it is none other than Jesus Christ himself. And thus Christ's "image" can be seen in Ecclesiastes in the following ways:

(i) The Need for a *Historical* Revelation of God

The prototype of modern man is 'doubting Thomas,' who said of the risen Jesus, 'Unless I see in his hands the print of the nails, and place my finger in the mark of the nails, and place my hand in his side, I will not believe' (Jn. 20:25). As we know, Jesus did not reject Thomas's demand as improper, but satisfied it, and so Thomas believed.[26]

What Heinz Zahrnt fails to mention in this statement is that Thomas himself has an Old Testament prototype, Ecclesiastes, who can tell us: "Satisfaction with what can be seen is better than getting carried away by dreams" (6:9). Israel's knowledge of God was always based on *visible* acts of God in history. "When the Old Testament is allowed to speak for itself," says von Rad, "it always confronts us with an event, an act of God either past or future."[27] Likewise Ecclesiastes, even though he lives in a "world

devoid of all action of Jahweh in history, . . . yet betrays that he is a last descendant of the people of Jahweh, since he knows that everything would be different if Jahweh's action, his work, were revealed to man (8:17, 11:5)."[28] It is simply assumed by Israel in general and Ecclesiastes in particular that if any further revelation of God takes place, it must occur in a *visible action of God in the world*. And thus Ecclesiastes, by being so supremely dependent on his eyes, is again an apt personification not only of Israel as a whole but also of modern man. For as Rudolf Bultmann has pointed out, "The only idea of God which is possible for modern man is that which can . . . seek and find the *unconditional in the conditional*, the beyond in this world, the transcendent in the here and now."[29] Ecclesiastes' great desire for a further historical revelation of God is almost too close to his heart to be spoken. Instead it stands silently behind *everything* he says. Even his cry, "Vanity of vanities, all is vanity," has "in it the implicit challenge [for God] to show himself in his original life of action in history in order that in the midst of disillusionment men may experience the full joy of being shown to be wrong by a new act of God which will drive this disillusionment from the field" (Miskotte).[30] Like his fellow sufferer Job, Ecclesiastes could easily have said of God:

Oh, that I knew where I might find him! . . . I go forward, but he is not there; and backward, but I cannot perceive him; on the left hand I seek him, but I cannot behold him; I turn to the right hand, but I cannot see him. (Job 23:3, 8, 9)

Like the New Testament's Simeon, Ecclesiastes is literally *"looking* for the consolation of Israel"; his eyes yearn to *see* God's salvation (Lk. 2:25, 30). The common plea of Israel, Ecclesiastes and modern man is, "Show us the Father, and we will be satisfied." Jesus' reply to this request was and is, "He who has seen *me* has seen the Father" (Jn. 14:8, 9). In order to make clear that this "me" is fully historical and is not a mere symbol for *anything else*, say a dreamy idealism or an abstract philosophy of life, the same Gospel writer can go on to describe this *"me" as* "that . . . which we have seen with our eyes, which we have looked upon and touched with our hands . . ." (1 Jn. 1:1). St. John also relates how "Philip found Nathanael, and said to him, 'We have found him of whom Moses in the law and also the prophets wrote, Jesus of Nazareth, the son of Joseph.'" If Ecclesiastes had been standing close by he would have been as skeptical and "guileless" as Nathanael, and probably would have quoted his saying, "Satisfaction with what can be seen is better than getting carried away by dreams." But when Nathanael asked, "Can anything good come out of Nazareth?" no doubt Ecclesiastes' heart would have skipped a beat upon hearing Philip's reply: "Come and see" (Jn. 1:45-47).

(ii) The Need for the Historical Yet *Absolute* Revelation of God

The questions Ecclesiastes asks of God are so all-inclusive in depth and breadth that it is obvious he could not possibly be satisfied with "just another" revelation of God in history. The revelation he is looking for must be decisive, absolute, once and for all. But because Ecclesiastes is looking for an *absolute historical* revelation of God, this revelation must be absolute in two ways: First, just because it is "revelation," it must communicate *knowledge* of God. It must include a word, or words, spoken about God. This word, or these words, if they are to be absolutely true, must not be subject to "time and chance," to the "vanity" of the world in the way all other things are. Nothing in time stays. The laws of time and chance say of everything under the sun—"Here today, gone tomorrow." There is a time for *this*, but its time soon passes; there is a time for *that*, but it too will pass away. And in the same way that all *things* are finite and transient, all "truths" are only relatively true. What Ecclesiastes is looking for, then, is a word from God that will carry with it a promise such as the one made by Jesus: "Heaven and earth will pass away, but my words will not pass away" (Mt. 24:35). Second, this absolute truth of God must be com-municated to man through a *single* historical event that is itself absolute. As we have seen, the restlessness of Ecclesiastes' mind, and of the Israelite mind in general, will not allow them to be satisfied with an abstract truth—a truth that is only a rarefied intellectualization, a bloodless and feeble "belief" that has no hard, bodily stuff attached to it. "Truth" for Israel is imparted in a definite, datable historical event or is not im-parted at all. For only in this way can one actu-ally know where to look for truth or how to "get in touch" with it. But in the Old Testament there are many such concrete, historical "truths." Therefore neither will "truths" finally satisfy the mind that is hell-bent to get once and for all to *the truth*. For it was part of Israel's genius to know that she could not, at any one time, live before a plurality of Gods or truths. "Hear, O Israel: The Lord our God, the Lord is one" is central to the faith of the Old as well as the New Testament (Deut. 6:4; Mk. 12:29). Therefore, since the God who reveals himself only through history is *one*, Israel's thought moves relentlessly toward *one single* decisive historical revelation of God. Here again Ecclesiastes is like a photog-rapher, for what he is searching for in this way is no less than *the* "focal point" of all history. We owe the use of this term to von Rad:

> On the basis of the Old Testament itself, it is truly difficult to answer the question of the unity of that Testament, for it has no focal-point such as found in the New. . . . It is, then, impossible to speak of a focal-point within the Old Testament which might have served as a constant standard for Israel. But the situation in the Old Testament does cor-respond to the view variously expressed in the New that the true goal of God's relationship with Israel is the coming of Jesus Christ. . . . Of course, it can be said that Jahweh [God] is the focal point of the Old Testament. This is, however, simply the begin-ning of the whole question: what kind of Jahweh is he?[31]

The problem, as Ecclesiastes sees it, is that "God is in heaven and we are on earth" (5:2). There-fore what he is looking for is a go-between, a decisive and normative revelation which will act as a mediator between these two extremes, the heavenly and the earthly.

(iii) The Need for the Divine Person

Ecclesiastes' need to find the focal point of all history, "the still point of the turning world," the single point which will reveal *the* truth of God, is expressed in the way in which he asks, "Who?" All of the deeply penetrating questions with which Ecclesiastes probes for meaning in the world begin with the question of "Who?" (3:21, 22; 6:12; 7:13, 24; 8:7; 10:14). Never does he ask "*How* do we know?" or "*Where* can we learn?" or "*What* can help us?" His questioning is always directed toward a person—a "Who." And in this quest, Ecclesiastes is again in perfect harmony with all the other voices of the Old Testament. Old Testament prophecy, says Zimmerli, "is not fulfilled in the literal sense of the coming to pass of a prediction that can be documented in individual occurrences after the manner of the fortune-teller; but it is indeed fulfilled in the promise of the divine person, about which all Old Testament promise revolves. . . ."[32] "Man," says Karl Barth, "will have to do with one Man as God's representative. . . . Of this the Old Testament is aware. . . ."[33] And thus all of the needs of Ecclesiastes that we have discussed thus far are combined and satisfied in "the divine person": In a "person" he would find the "body and blood" of a *historical* event; in "divine" he would find a historical yet *absolute* event; and in "the" he would find the *unity* of the single historical yet absolute event. Also in a "person" Ecclesiastes would find one who could communicate the *meaning* of such an event. For he still has needs to be met in the things that he wants to *know*. His search for *the divine person* is a search for the one "who can tell us . . ." (6:12; 8:7; 10:14).

(iv) The Need for the Divine Person Who Can Tell Us—"What Kind of God?"

Ecclesiastes, like St. Paul, was a "Hebrew born of Hebrews." In any case, he is certainly representative of all of the hopes of the people of the Old Testament. These hopes, and the way they are fulfilled in Christ, are neatly gathered up and summarized in the following first few words of the New Testament's Letter to the Hebrews:

When in former times God spoke to our forefathers, he spoke in fragmentary and varied fashion through the prophets. But in this final age, he has spoken to us in the Son whom he has made heir to the whole universe, and through whom he created all orders of existence: the Son who is the effulgence of God's splendour and the stamp of God's very being, and sustains the universe by his word of power. When he had brought about the purgation of sins, he took his seat at the right hand of Majesty on high. . . . (Heb. 1:1-3 NEB)

The first thing we learn about "What kind of God" from such a statement is "What kind of man" this God is dealing with. Ecclesiastes would have approved of Kierkegaard's remark that God will not send his *personal* representative into the world "in order to make trivial remarks." Why? Because Ecclesiastes is in perfect agreement with all of the rest of the Bible that without *radically* new help from the outside, man's situation is radically desperate and hopeless. Ecclesiastes—as one who "reads much, is a great observer, and looks quite through the deeds of men"—knows that man is not only trapped in his ignorance about God but is also trapped in his stubborn tendency to disregard what he *can* know of God. In other words, man needs help in the worst way and Ecclesiastes is quite sure that this help cannot be found *within* man himself. For "all men are in the same predicament—the hearts of men are full of evil [and] madness fills their hearts while they live" (9:3). This is the basis for his doleful lament that "There is nothing new under the sun!" If any real help is to come into this situation, it will have to mean a totally new breakthrough into the closed circle of man's isolation from the knowledge and service of God. Says O. S. Rankin:

The pessimism of Koheleth in regard to the value of what the world has to offer to man is not alien to Christian thought. . . . this book is at least at one with Christianity in its rejection of a confident humanism. Koheleth reads with uncanny insight the hearts and thoughts of his fellow men. Jesus also, according to John 2:25, "knew what was in man." Along with the poet of Job, Koheleth has the distinction of investigating a problem which besets mankind in general and for which there is no easy solution—indeed no solution offered by human resources.[34]

This means, then, that any divine person who comes to remedy *this* situation must come from a point outside of the world with its "human resources," must come from no less than God himself and will therefore be men's *Savior* and the mediator of a *new* covenant between God and men.

"Only on this background," says Tillich of Ecclesiastes' realistic appraisal of man, "the message of Jesus as the Christ has meaning. Only if we accept an honest view of the human situation, of man's old reality, can we understand the message that in Christ a new reality has appeared. He who never has said about his life 'Vanity of vanities, all is vanity' cannot honestly say with Paul, 'In these things we are more than conquerors through him who loved us.' "[35] These last few words of St. Paul bring us to the *first* question Ecclesiastes would ask the divine person about "what kind of God." To use Ecclesiastes' own words: "This I saw and clearly understood: that the righteous and the wise and all that they do are controlled by God's hand. *But whether behind this control there is love or hate—no man knows*" (9:1). Here again Ecclesiastes is an eloquent spokesman for present-day man. For according to Heinz Zahrnt, in his book *What Kind of God?* the "secret longing" for modern man is

for the silent apathy of the universe to be overcome, for men to be reconciled through love—but not through love which simply remains suspended in heaven as an eternal idea or broods over the waters like a spirit, but by a love which becomes a reality here upon earth and is involved in history, which suffers with men and shares their fate.[36]

And thus it is apparent that what Ecclesiastes and modern man are here both demanding of God has actually occurred in the life and death of Jesus of Nazareth. Nothing could be more obvious than the fact that every sentence in the New Testament witnesses to what St. Paul calls "the love of God made visible in Jesus Christ" (Rom. 8:39 *The Jerusalem Bible*).

But what does this love mean to me personally and especially what does it mean in terms of my *future*? This question, which preoccupied Ecclesiastes, is the *second* question he is asking about "what kind of God." Ecclesiastes lived during that period of Israel's history when her people were beginning to ask more and more seriously with Job: "If a man die, shall he live again?" (Job 14:14). Or as Ecclesiastes could express the same question: "Who can tell man what will follow after his time under the sun?" (6:12). "That, truly," says Arthur Cochrane, "is the question for which Ecclesiastes (and the Old Testament as a whole) has no answer."[37] Ironically, this question about death was raised even more intensely for Ecclesiastes because of his love for life:

Truly light is sweet! And it is pleasant for the eyes to see the sun. And therefore if a man lives many years, let him enjoy all of them. For let him remember that the days of darkness will be many. All that is to come is emptiness. (11:7, 8)

As Eichrodt says of death, " . . . *in Israel* men shrink from this threat to life *all the more*. . . . Precisely because men have learned to know this God as the giver of life, his No to life shakes them to the very roots of their being."[38] Thus Ecclesiastes, just because of the enjoyment he found in living obediently before God, would have understood Nietzsche's statement that "All joy wants eternity."[39] But the fact that Nietzsche was no pious Israelite should indicate to us that it is not just the men of Israel for whom "the undiscovered country" of death is a real problem and threat. A careful study of human existence, says theologian Carl Braaten, "will disclose that man is by nature one who hopes for fulfillment beyond death."[40]

But it is also true that men by nature do not like to face or even to think about death, and theologians are no exception. Many modern theologians have tried to pretend that the problem of death does not even exist and have considered it the height of theological bad manners if anyone should raise the question of what—if anything—lies "beyond death." Given over entirely to a superficial "relevance," modern theology has considered death irrelevant to life—life alone being "where it's really at." But this situation is now fast changing largely because theologians have begun to see just how relevant to life the problem of death can be—and not just to the life of the individual but also to the life of any society as a whole. This is one of the reasons why we are now beginning to see more and more references to Ecclesiastes in the writings of contemporary philosophers and theologians. For the questions raised by death are absolutely crucial to the thought of Ecclesiastes. He does not flinch from death's harsh reality but meets its challenge as courageously as any man before him or since. "The problem of death," says Anderson, "—the most universally human experience—hangs like a dark shadow over the whole book."[41] Ecclesiastes is preoccupied by this darkness because he knows with Zahrnt that "death is not simply a matter of our own individual dying but is a shadow of transitoriness which lies over the whole world":

Consequently, any theology which . . . takes so seriously its concern for our fellow men and its responsibility for the world . . . in making the earth a 'home,' is bound to face the question of death. Otherwise all creative and formative activity in the world is like water that beats up against the coast and falls back again, constantly rising and falling, endlessly moving backwards and forwards. Death seems to make everything uncertain: at first it looks as though it is worth while to work and be busy —and then it turns into nothing. 'All is vanity and is striving after wind,' is the conclusion of Ecclesiastes as he weighs up his observations about the world; this is wisdom in the face of death, the wisdom of death. Thus . . . all honest and profound consideration of life is a rendez-vous, or rather a battle with death.[42]

Ecclesiastes knows there can never be a real,

final hope for man unless man first faces and fully takes into account the utter hopelessness of death. Hence the new "philosophers and theologians of hope," from Bloch to Moltmann, find themselves constantly returning to Ecclesiastes for a perfect expression of the exact problem with which they are all wrestling. Moltmann, for instance, can begin his book *Religion, Revolution and the Future* by saying:

"Nothing new happens under the sun," says Ecclesiastes. "Hence all is vanity." In saying this he expressed that wisdom of resignation which can make man melancholy as well as serene. But if there can be nothing new in the world, there is also no real future. And if there is no future, there is also no real history. If there is no history, our world is not open, but shut in. Without history, man, too, is not a being who is open and full of questions and hopes for the future, but one who is enclosed and imprisoned in himself.[43]

It soon becomes clear that in Ecclesiastes we have a foreshadowing of the modern "theologian of hope." Even "in Eccles. 3:10 and following, where the word 'hope' is not expressly present," says Zimmerli, "we are clearly dealing with the problem of the future and the possibility of man taking hold of the future."[44] For even when he is most pessimistic about man's life and its possibilities, Ecclesiastes negatively mirrors the positive hope for man's future in God, the same future the Christian faith believes to have been fulfilled and further revealed in Jesus the Christ, namely, the resurrection of the dead.

But the claim that man does have a future beyond death only raises a *third* and really crucial question for Ecclesiastes: What kind of future is it? One thing should be clear from the beginning: Ecclesiastes would have no use for a life on the other side of death which has the purpose of "rewarding the good and punishing the evil." As Eichrodt has said of the Old Testament's dawning hope for life after death:

It is *not primarily the idea of retribution* which leads to a postulate of a resurrection of the dead. . . . *hope of a revelation of God's glory* plays an incomparably more important part. . . . It is *not so much the question of the moral ordering of the world which drives men to such a prayer* [Isa. 26:19]—there is no judgment of the dead—as *suffering under the limitless dominion of death,* which threatens to give the lie to God's universal design, and to destroy the hope of the coming salvation.[45]

As we have already seen, Ecclesiastes is a man intoxicated by the sheer Godness of God. Since God is in control of absolutely everything that occurs under the sun, man is in no way "the master of his own fate, the captain of his own soul." At the same time, Ecclesiastes is obviously well aware of the inequalities that God himself has subjected men to. "Life itself is unfair," as John F. Kennedy once remarked. Ecclesiastes can see this "unfairness" clearly enough. Who, for instance, is in control of the circumstances of his birth, his "time to be born"? But Ecclesiastes can further see that because God is the ruler of *all* of life, *God* is also behind all of life's "unfairnesses":

For God gives wisdom and knowledge and enjoyment to whomever he pleases; but to another man God gives the task of gathering possessions which are then only handed over to whomever God wishes. This also is incomprehensible and like chasing the wind. (2:26)

It is incomprehensible enough to Ecclesiastes that God allows this state of affairs to continue now, in this lifetime. But to say that God will later raise men from the dead only in order to subject them to more of the same unequal treatment would be a thought absolutely unthinkable to Ecclesiastes. Ecclesiastes clearly believes in "predestination" (3:1, 9, 14, 15; 6:10-11; 7:14; 11:5). But the idea that God predestines some men to salvation and others to eternal damnation would no doubt prompt him to say with Milton, "I may go to hell, but such a God will never command my respect."[46] And there is no doubt that modern man also stands firmly with Milton at this point. Obviously, the only way belief in an "eternal hell" can ever be maintained is to remove God from responsibility for everlasting punishment by making *man* the fall guy. This

is done by claiming that man is finally free to decide his own eternal destiny, is the free master of his own fate, the captain of his own soul. But for Ecclesiastes, as well as for the New Testament, this view is idolatrous; it is tantamount to attributing deity to man, as we have already seen. If man finally can choose his own destiny, man is finally his own master and hence finally his own God—it is as simple as that.

If Ecclesiastes were to show up in the world today, and the "orthodox" view of "Heaven or hell—the choice is yours!" were held out to him as a true representation of the Christian faith, he would turn his back on it. Because of this monstrous distortion of God's love made visible in Christ, Ecclesiastes would continue to look elsewhere for meaning in life; and in this search he would join the great majority of other "modern men," men who have also rejected "the good news" because it has never been presented to them as being really good enough. With Camus, Ecclesiastes would reject the kind of god that has come into the world "with dissatisfaction and a preference for futile sufferings."[47] And with the same tough-minded honesty, he would see with Camus that "Christians"

have hoisted [Christ] on to a judge's bench, in the secret of their hearts, and they smite, above all they judge, they judge in his name. He spoke softly to the adulteress: "Neither do I condemn thee!" but that doesn't matter; they condemn without absolving anyone. . . . they believe solely in sin, never in grace.[48]

Any key to understanding Ecclesiastes will include the little word "all." "All" is especially appropriate in describing his view of God's sovereignty or omnipotence: "God alone brings *all* things about . . ." (3:14). "The righteous and the wise and *all* that they do are controlled by God's hand" (9:1). "You cannot know what is in the mind of God, who does *all*" (11:5).

This means, then, that if God should also be revealed to be a God of *love,* and furthermore the claim is made that God wishes to save men by raising them from the dead into *everlasting life,* Ecclesiastes could never conceive of this happening unless it happened to *all* men. Ecclesiastes is so thoroughly convinced of God's absolute and omnipotent control over *all* that occurs, that if he were also convinced that God "desires all men to be saved and come to the knowledge of the truth" (1 Tim. 2:4), then he would necessarily believe that indeed *all* men *will* be saved and come to the knowledge of the truth. And thus any denial of God's universal salvation of all men must mean that either God *cannot* save the work of his own hands and hence he is not infinite in power, or else he does not *wish* to save all men and hence he is not infinite in love. This is why belief in an "eternal hell" always makes a mockery of either God's power or love, and thus mocks the God who is infinite in both.

But no amount of wishful thinking on the part of Ecclesiastes or anyone else can make the good news of God's universal salvation true. If it is true it must be attested by one with the authority to do so. Therefore God's good news goes one step further: In the *historical* person of his son, God has given us the visible key, the flesh and blood way through which we may now *know* this promise is true by even now beginning to enjoy, through faith in Jesus as the Christ, the "first fruits" of this great joy which will ultimately come to *all* people. And therefore the great, triumphal "*alls*" made certain only by the New Testament's Christ are truly the *alls* of the really *good* news that Ecclesiastes longs to hear:

Behold, I bring you good news of a great joy which will come to *all* the people; for to you is born . . . a Saviour, who is Christ the Lord. (Lk. 2:10-11)

Jesus answered, . . . "I, when I am lifted up from the earth, will draw all men to myself. (Jn. 12:32)

Then as one man's trespass led to condemnation for all men, so one man's act of righteousness leads to acquittal and life for all men. (Rom. 5:18)

For since it was a man who brought death into the world, a man also brought resurrection of the dead. As in Adam all men die, so in Christ all will be brought to life; but each in his own proper place: Christ the firstfruits, and afterwards, at his coming,

those who belong to Christ. Then comes the end, when he delivers up the kingdom to God the Father, after abolishing every kind of domination, authority, and power. For he is destined to reign until God has put all enemies under his feet; and the last enemy to be abolished is death. . . . then the Son himself will also be made subordinate to God who made all things subject to him, and thus God will be all in all. (1 Cor. 15:22-26, 28 NEB)

For he has made known to us in all wisdom and insight the mystery of his will, according to his purpose which he set forth in Christ as a plan for the fullness of time, to unite all things in him, things in heaven and things on earth. (Eph. 1:9-10)

Through [Christ] God chose to reconcile the whole universe to himself, making peace through the shedding of his blood upon the cross—to reconcile all things, whether on earth or in heaven, through him alone. (Col. 1:20 NEB)

This is good, and it is acceptable in the sight of God our Saviour, who desires all men to be saved and to come to the knowledge of the truth. For there is one God, and there is one mediator between God and men, the man Christ Jesus, who gave himself as a ransom for all. . . . (1 Tim. 2:3-6)

Jesus Christ . . . is himself the remedy for the defilement of our sins, not our sins only but the sins of all the world. (1 Jn. 2:2 NEB)

For God has consigned all men to disobedience, that he may have mercy on all. O the depth of the riches and wisdom and knowledge of God! How unsearchable are his judgments and how inscrutable his ways! "For . . . who has given a gift to him that he might be repaid?" For from him and through him and to him are all things. To him be glory forever. Amen. (Rom. 11:32-36)

And thus Ecclesiastes' discernment of the vanity encompassing *all* men will find a satisfying answer only in a redemption of man that is likewise *all*-embracing. This is why Vischer can ask, "If the Preacher is not right that all is vanity and there is nothing new under the sun . . . why did Christ descend from God's throne, and die on a cross to redeem the whole world?"[49]

Ecclesiastes, like all the other biblical writers, is keenly aware of the *positive* aspect of suffering, the "goodness of grief," the grief that can turn men to the true God by constantly accompanying the worship of false gods. "When life is sweet, enjoy it; but when life is hard remember this: God has brought about the one as well as the other in order to prevent man from finding any created thing completely trustworthy" (7:14; cf. 3:14; 7:2-6). But Ecclesiastes also knows this answer is incomplete, for it still does not answer the "Why?" of suffering: not only why has God made suffering *the* necessary pathway to knowledge of him? But also why does God subject some men to suffering without enabling them to benefit from it at all, as in the case of obviously innocent children who suffer and die? For Ecclesiastes is quite clear that God is ultimately behind all the suffering in the world: "Oh, what miserable futility God himself has subjected the family of man to" (1:13b; cf. 3:9-10). And the New Testament agrees. Indeed Plumptre[50] believes St. Paul may have had Ecclesiastes' above statement in mind when he wrote: "For the created universe . . . was made victim of frustration not by its own choice, but because God subjected it" (Rom. 8:19-20 NEB). A cross can be seen in the picture I have used to illustrate this "Why?" (8:14). And this should indicate that the Christian, like Ecclesiastes, has no answer for this question. The answer the Christian has does not remove the "Why?" but it does overcome it. It removes the bitterness of this question's sting by pointing to its final, happy resolution: "For I reckon that the sufferings we now endure bear no comparison with the splendour, as yet unrevealed, which is in store for us," as St. Paul could put it (Rom. 8:18 NEB). But unless this "us" finally includes *all* men, then either man is his own master and God is not God, or else "the good news" is not so "good" after all.

(v) The Need for *Faith* in the Divine Person

When the risen Christ fulfilled Thomas' demand to "see in his hands the print of the nails, and place my finger in the mark of the nails," Thomas then exclaimed, "My Lord and my God!" But Jesus replied: "Have you believed because you have seen me? Blessed are those who have not seen and yet believe" (Jn. 20:26-29). We have also seen how Ecclesiastes, too, literally *looked*, with his eyes, for the consolation of Israel. But this does not mean that Ecclesiastes ever expected—even if "the divine person" should appear—to be more a man of sight than of faith. At his book's conclusion, Ecclesiastes recommends letting "Your heart and your eyes show you the way," and it is no accident that he gives first place to the heart in this twofold way (11:9). The questions asked by Ecclesiastes clearly point to the need of men's eyes, the need to *see* God's own "incarnation" in visible space and time. But even if this historical event should take place, God would still demand that men have faith in him and hence faith in his own *incarnation*. But faith, precisely in order to remain faith, always requires the relinquishing of all props and proofs, as we have already seen. And thus we return to von Rad's statement that even when God reveals himself in history, he "continually retreats" from men in order "that they only have the gamble of faith to rest on."[51] This means that even in God's self-revelation in Jesus, God is still "hidden." Though history tells us unmistakably that Jesus was a real person who came visibly into the world, faith is still necessary to tell us unmistakably that he is *the divine* person. As Zahrnt puts it:

Even if God reveals himself in the world, his concealment does not stop. In his revelation he is to be found in things that are indistinguishable from other things in the world: the Bible is a book, Jesus of Nazareth a rabbi, the church an institution and the Christian an ordinary man.[52]

Because Ecclesiastes knows that in this world it is only *faith* in God that can satisfy men's deepest longings, he thereby stands in the tradition of Isaiah in anticipating the divine person's *lowliness*.[53] This becomes clear when we remember that by asking God for a final, *historical* revelation of himself, he thereby is also asking God to subject himself to "vanity." By asking God to take on visible, historical *flesh*, he is also asking God to subject himself to all of the humiliating "vanity" of flesh, including death. For only if

God comes into the world *visibly* and *in humiliation* can Ecclesiastes' "two ways" of the eyes and the heart be satisfied—visibly to satisfy his eyes, but also in stripped and lowly flesh in order that the heart's gamble of faith will have *nothing other than this man alone* to rest on. In this way, then, Ecclesiastes would seem to anticipate the very essence of the New Testament's view of Jesus:

The divine nature was his from the first; yet he did not prize his equality with God, but made himself nothing, assuming the nature of a slave. Bearing the human likeness, revealed in human shape, he humbled himself, and in obedience accepted even death—death on a cross. (Phil. 2:6-8 NEB)

Thus in Ecclesiastes we can see that no man can really find peace in life unless he has first made his peace with death; and further that no man can *really* make peace with death unless it is made through faith in the One who fought and conquered for *all* men, Jesus Christ. But here again "faith" means that all props and proofs must go—including "proofs from Scripture"! We have tried to show that all of the great questions of the Old Testament are boiled down and distilled into their clearest, simplest and most concentrated form in Ecclesiastes. But the fact that these questions then correspond so accurately to the New Testament's answers does not really prove anything. To accept this kind of argument as proof that Jesus is the Christ would be to place one's faith in a mere argument rather than in Jesus himself. What this kind of argument can do, however, is to help clarify what *the question* of all mankind then was and now is. For without such a clarification we can never fully understand or appreciate what the New Testament's *answer* was and is. It is true that the New Testament itself uses a kind of "proof from Scripture" or "proof from prophecy." Jesus himself could say, "If you believed Moses, you would believe me, for he wrote of me" (Jn. 5:46). Nevertheless, says Zimmerli, "Christ will never permit himself to be 'deduced' from the Old Testament promise-material, which is of such diverse expression. . . . This does not ex-

clude the fact that faith in Christ afterwards recognizes in the Old Testament a book full of genuine allusions to Jesus Christ." It is then in terms of this "ultimate purpose," concludes Zimmerli, the purpose of bringing men to faith, that all New Testament "proofs from scripture" are to be understood.[54]

Is it then impossible to prove from scripture that Jesus is the Christ? Yes; for this proof is given only by the Holy Spirit. The question of the truth of Christianity can be decided only by faith and the election of grace. It is, however, to this decision that the proof from scripture leads. (Vischer)[55]

But Ecclesiastes can help us understand what is meant even by this "decision of faith." For he begins his quest by asking, "What is best for men to *do* during their few days of life under the sun?" (2:3). And this is faith's question because faith is believing and believing is *doing*. So what does faith do? As St. Augustine puts it, "Love God and do as you please!" That is, faith is free to do absolutely *anything* it pleases as long as *everything* it does is directed toward the single goal of fulfilling the hungry, Christ-shaped vacuum of all men's hearts, the vacuum represented so perfectly by Ecclesiastes. Ordinary human love and justice are "vanity." They will grow weary and deteriorate into far less than love and justice unless they are nourished by a love far greater than the weak and fickle love mere men are capable of.

Ecclesiastes correctly sees that his own job boils down quite simply to casting upon the waters—that is, far and wide and indiscriminately—whatever nourishing bread he can (11:1). The Christian's job likewise is simply to "spread the bread." But because of its faith in the divine person, the New Testament's bread—the very bread Ecclesiastes hungered for—is infinitely "improved" in both quality and quantity. And therefore Jesus answers the question of "what must we *do*?" by pointing to himself as the divine nourishment which must be given to the world: "This is the work God requires: believe in the one whom he has sent . . . . The bread that God gives is he who comes down from heaven and brings life to the world . . . . I am the bread of life. Whoever comes to me shall never be hungry, and whoever believes in me shall never be thirsty" (Jn. 6:28, 29, 33, 35).

3. *Two Remaining Questions*

[Ecclesiastes] puts the logic of a non-Christian position with tremendous force, to all who feel keenly the misery of the world. More vividly than anything else in the Old Testament, it shows us how imperious was the necessity for the revelation of God in Christ.[56]

If this statement by A. S. Peake is true, and we believe it is, then two important questions are suggested by it:

a. If Ecclesiastes does make so utterly clear the necessity for God's revelation in Christ, then why does the New Testament not refer to Ecclesiastes or quote from him? The first and most obvious answer to this question lies in Ecclesiastes' *authority* at the time the New Testament was written. For the New Testament writers were careful to back up their "arguments from Scripture" only with those writings of undisputed authority and influence. For the most part, this meant "the Law and the Prophets." Ecclesiastes, relatively speaking, was a young upstart among the biblical writers; therefore the safe thing to do in bolstering an argument with particular passages of Scripture was to stick to the old tried-and-true favorites. For it was not until the so-called "Synod of Jamnia"—about A.D. 100—that the rabbis finally decided, not without much dispute, that Ecclesiastes did indeed belong in the Hebrew Bible. It should also be said, however, that although the New Testament writers did not choose to make overt use of Ecclesiastes (as the early church fathers did), they easily could have. For as von Rad points out, the New Testament writers

found in every part of [the old writings] testimonies which could be applied to their own theological, Christological, and ecclesiological arguments. . . . Although the New Testament shows a freedom and breadth and vitality in interpreting the Old Testament such as the Church has hardly ever achieved since, all the possible ways of relating the Old Testament to Jesus and his Church are far from being exhausted by it.[57]

The second thing to be said about the fact that Ecclesiastes is nowhere explicitly used in the New Testament is that it is used implicitly. Some scholars are willing to say that its use is even a bit more than implied,[58] for there are many passages in the New Testament that sound as though they might have been cribbed from the Preacher. For example, when St. James tells us that "you are a mist that appears for a time and then vanishes" (4:14), he is not being exactly original. And it "is in remarkable agreement with the verdict of Ecclesiastes," says Karl Barth, that St. Paul can say, "the form of this world is passing away" (1 Cor. 7:31).[59]

But by searching for specific references to Ecclesiastes in the New Testament, we are really in danger of not seeing the wood for the trees. It is like the anecdote of the man who bet a visitor to his home that he, his friend, could not find the name of a certain location which appeared on a large map hanging on the wall of his study. After searching carefully for a full hour, his friend was convinced that such a name was not on the map. But the map's owner then pointed to the large faint letters which made up almost the complete background of the map. And so it is with Ecclesiastes in the New Testament. More than any other book in the Old Testament, Ecclesiastes epitomizes that skeptical period in Israel's history which forms the dark background against which the light of the New Testament can be clearly contrasted and understood and appreciated. It is for this very reason, for example, that Ronald Knox, in attempting to define the essential difference between the two Testaments, finds it necessary to refer to Ecclesiastes: "The difference between the Old and the New Testaments is the difference between a man who said 'There is nothing new under the sun' and a God who says 'Behold, I make all things new.' "[60]

b. The second and final question is more important because it relates to the "one thing needful" in our own time. It is this: If the New Testament's answer is so "made to order" for Ecclesiastes' question (as we have argued), and Ecclesiastes' question is so similar to the question modern man is asking (as we have also argued), then why is it that modern man is apparently so unreceptive to the New Testament's answer? That is, if the "non-Christian position" of modern man, like Ecclesiastes, also shows us how "imperious" is the necessity for God's revelation in Christ, and this revelation has already occurred, then why is it not more readily accepted? Certainly part of the answer to this question is to be found in Ecclesiastes' own pessimistic assessment of man and the shortness of his memory: "For the men of today do not remember yesterday, just as the men of tomorrow will not remember today" (1:11). But this "answer" is really just another way of stating the question: If our time, like that of Ecclesiastes, is such an open vacuum in search of meaning, then why is our time not fulfilled by the very One who came into the world to fulfill such vacuums, just as the coming of Christ did indeed fulfill the vacuum represented by Ecclesiastes? Why, as Gabriel Vahanian puts it, is it "easier to make the conversion from pre-Christian to Christian than it is from post-Christian to Christian"?[61]

Ecclesiastes himself points us to the answer to this question when he says:

I said to myself, "God will judge the righteous and the wicked, for there is with God an appointed time for every intention and every deed." In this [wicked] behavior of men, I reflected, God is limiting them in order to show them their own finitude and their bestial behavior to each other. (3:17, 18)

This means, first of all, that though man is always totally dependent upon God's own timing and judgment to straighten him out, there *will* be a time of judgment for both the church and modern man, for "the righteous and the wicked." And "judgment" means that things will necessarily get much worse before they can get better.

Generally speaking, however, things will get worse for modern man, for "the world," before they get worse for the church. Why? Because God always judges and reforms the church *through* the world, just as he always judged and reformed Israel *through* the pagan nations surrounding her. Today the growing "godlessness" of the world is God's judgment upon the church. The growing assumption among modern men that "God is dead" is, as Zahrnt says,

a judgment on theology and the church, and therefore a call to repentance. . . . The negative side lies in the fact of the constant limitation of the sphere in which belief in God is operative. But the result of the positive aspect which accompanies it is that thought and language about God has been purified and made more profound, undergoing a continual process of cleansing. . . . Properly understood . . . modern atheism . . . has had a purifying and refining effect on theology. Think of the things we took for God! Think of the things we claimed to be the work of God! Think of the things we have said and done in the name of God! How often have we made God in our own image! From now on, this kind of idolatry is impossible. The positive achievement of modern atheism is the vigorous purification which Christianity, together with its theology, has undergone, bringing the rejection of every kind of idolatry. The French Christian Jean Lacroix once expressed this in the words: "I am grateful to my atheist friends, for they have taught me not to cheat."[62]

We would question whether Christianity and theology are yet even close to being as "pure" as Zahrnt seems to think. This is why we believe that things must still get much worse before they can get better. But there is no doubt that Zahrnt has correctly spotted the direction in which the church and the world are moving. And thus we return once more to the truth behind Bonhoeffer's statement that "The world that has come of age is more godless, and perhaps for that reason nearer to God, than the world before its coming of age." The growing godlessness of the world will force the church to trim, compress and simplify her message, to return to "first principles" and to strip herself of nonsense and historical clutter. In other words, the more modern man comes to resemble Ecclesiastes, with all of his tough realism, his blunt honesty, his no-nonsense questions, and his desperate cry of "Vanity of vanities!" the more the modern church will be forced to resemble the church of the New Testament, with all of its boldness, vitality and power. For "no book in the Old Testament so challenges Christian faith to meet the questions it asks" (Atkins).[63] This is why, as Rainey observes, that "among the books of the Bible Qoheleth has the distinction of being the most distrusted by the pious but best liked by the skeptic."[64] And therefore it will not be until the present fat and sleepy church is forced to become lean and hungry by "the new Ecclesiastes," modern man, that the church will once more become truly powerful and dangerous in the world. Just at that point when both the church and modern man come face to face with their own time to die, they will miraculously find also their time to be reborn. Until this time comes, modern men will listen less and less to an indistinct church babble vaguely of "truths," for they will know "damned well" (we use the term theologically) that they need the certainty of *the truth*. Nor will they listen to talk of an abstract truth, for they will damned well know they need a real down-to-earth, "flesh and blood," *historical* truth. They will have nothing but contempt for shallow little homilies about man and his own wonderful "freedom"; for their intuition will know damned well that unless help comes from something more trustworthy than men themselves, then they are lost. Nor will modern men be interested in the escapism of "pie in the sky by and by," but they will show keen interest in an "eternal life" that *is* capable of transforming and giving meaning to the present; for they will damned well know with Paul "if it is for this life only" that Christ has given Christians hope, then Christians "of all men are most to be pitied" (1 Cor. 15:19 NEB). And yet modern men will not be bullied by threats that God will later throw them into hell, because they will know damned well that the damnation they are *now* experiencing is quite enough to suffer at the hands of any "God of love." Nor will they be impressed by the church's childish activistic attempts to ingratiate herself to the world by pretending to something other than what she is—by pretending to be a worldly "swinger," a sociological or political sage, etc. Like another modern spokesman, atheist Albert Camus, modern men will know damned well that the world needs real dialogue . . . and that the only possible dialogue is the kind between people who remain what they are and speak their minds. This is tantamount to saying that the world of today needs Christians who remain Christians. . . . The grouping we need is a grouping of men resolved to speak out clearly and to pay up personally.[65]

When all of this happens, modern man will truly and fully be the soul-brother of Ecclesiastes. The "time" of Ecclesiastes himself will once more be upon us; and the job of Ecclesiastes is to "Prepare the way of the Lord, to make his paths straight" (Mt. 3:3). For it is only by facing up to the purifying force and clarity of the *true* questions of Ecclesiastes that the church's answers can be made correspondingly true and forceful and clear. Whenever the church's answers are not informed by "the fine hammered steel of woe," by precisely the same hard and deep questions Ecclesiastes asks, its "answers" will be superficial, uncertain and deservedly ignored.

Within that body of sacred writings we have come to know as "the Bible," Ecclesiastes is the diamond. It is small and beautiful and multifaceted, and there is absolutely nothing harder or more solidly compressed: a compression resulting from having been formed at—and a hardness enabling it to cut a straight path to—the depths of the world. In any case, the better we become acquainted with this astonishing little masterpiece, the more difficult it becomes to dispute Melville's assertion that "the truest of all books . . . is Ecclesiastes."

Notes

PART I

1. Eugene O'Neill, *Long Day's Journey into Night* (New Haven: Yale University Press, 1956), p. 131.

2. Søren Kierkegaard, *The Last Years* (New York: Harper & Row, 1965), p. 350.

3. Dietrich Bonhoeffer, *Ethics* (London: Collins, 1964), pp. 68-69.

4. Melville, *Moby Dick* (New York: Modern Library, 1950), p. 535.

5. "Henri Cartier-Bresson on the Art of Photography," *Harper's Magazine*, November 1961, p. 74.

6. *Ibid.*, p. 75.

7. *Ibid.*, p. 74.

8. "Good Fisherman," *Newsweek,* July 22, 1968, p. 78.

9. "Henri Cartier-Bresson on the Art of Photography," *op. cit.*, p. 73.

10. *Ibid.*, p. 75.

11. Von Rad, *Old Testament Theology,* Vol. 1 (New York: Harper & Row, 1962), p. 458.

12. "Henri Cartier-Bresson on the Art of Photography," *op. cit.*, p. 74.

13. Michael Korda, "Cartier-Bresson Today—3 Views," *Popular Photography,* May 1967, p. 142.

14. A more literal translation of this verse is: "Vanity of vanities, says the Preacher, vanity of vanities! All is vanity" (RSV). However, the undoubted beauty of this more traditional and familiar rendering does nothing for the verse's meaning. For the fact is that "vanity," as it is here used by Ecclesiastes, is an archaic word for us today. I know from experience that "vanity" means little more to today's young people than excessive concern about one's appearance. *The New English* and *Anchor* Bibles make valiant attempts to overcome this problem by replacing "vanity" with "emptiness" and "vapor" respectively. But the equally obvious limitations of these terms have helped to convince me that there is no one word in modern English that does justice to the richness of the Hebrew word

hebel (literally a "vapor" or "breath"). This conclusion is further borne out by the long lists of "synonyms" invariably used by commentators in their attempts to convey the meaning of the one word *hebel*, or "vanity." What I have done, therefore, is to use, along with "vanity," six of the more "popular" of these synonyms. The variable use of several English words to denote this one Hebrew word will, I hope, serve not only to clarify *hebel's* meaning, but will also give me something of the same versatility with which Ecclesiastes used this single word to convey various shades of meaning.

Why stop at six synonyms when there is a much longer list to choose from? It is the Talmudic rabbis who save this cut-off point from being entirely arbitrary. For, they pointed out, if the plural ("vanities") is counted as two, then the word "vanity" is used seven times in the traditional translations of this famous verse. And thus, according to the rabbis, in the number seven "Koheleth was expressing a judgment on each day of creation; Koheleth was referring to seven stages in the growth and development of man, etc." (*The Bible Reader* [New York: The Bruce Publishing Co., 1969], pp. 397-398). If seven "vanities" could produce this kind of inspiration for these venerable men of old, then seven "vanities" are good enough for me!

In recent literature, the constant refrain of "So it goes" in Vonnegut's tragicomic novel *Slaughterhouse-Five* is a good illustration of what Ecclesiastes is getting at in *his* refrain of "This, also, is vanity."

15. This verse (along with 7:26) has often been translated in ways that would make Ecclesiastes seem to support the conventional but unrealistic teaching that God rewards good men with good luck and bad men with bad luck. But as Scott has commented, the verse "is simply a fuller statement of what has already been said about the inscrutable will of God and is to be understood in the light of 9:1-2." *Why* God blesses one man and not the other is to Ecclesiastes, as Scott says, "another of the baffling phenomena of life, as the concluding words of the verse show" (R. B. Y. Scott, *The Anchor Bible: Proverbs-Ecclesiastes* [Garden City: Doubleday and Company, Inc., 1965], p. 219). It is also helpful for the proper understanding of this verse if it is read in the light of 2:21 and 8:14.

16. For commentary on this famous poem of "the times and seasons" (3:1-9), see p. 86.

17. Most modern commentators agree that "to cast away stones" (RSV) is a euphemism for the act of marital intercourse. "Gathering stones" would then point to the time of refraining from this act.

18. This familiar verse is usually translated as "God has made everything *beautiful* in its time" (RSV). Most commentators are agreed, however, that here Ecclesiastes "unmistakably reflects Gen. 1" (Zimmerli, "The Place and Limit of the Wisdom in the Framework of the Old Testament Theology," *Scottish Journal of Theology*, Vol. 17 [1964], p. 155). "Unmistakably" for Zimmerli, perhaps. But in order to help "the average reader" avoid any mistake, I have chosen to use "good" in this verse, since it is evidently this important and often repeated word in the first chapter of Genesis (verses 4, 12, 18, 21, 25, 31) that is here summed up by Ecclesiastes as "beautiful." It is interesting that modern slang also uses "beautiful" as a strong form of "good"—e.g., "You're a beautiful kid, Charlie Brown!"

19. For commentary on this verse see p. 89.

20. This verse has been damaged in manuscript transmission and, as Scott says, any attempt to reconstruct it is "little more than a guess" (Scott, *The Anchor Bible, op. cit.*, p. 228). Most commentators agree however that in this verse, which follows the preceding verse's "hierarchy of man's oppression of man," Ecclesiastes apparently finds something positive to say in regard to this negative aspect of life. What could this "positive" be? In 4:4 he has already told us that a certain "positive" can be seen deriving from precisely the "negative" of greedy ambition: "I saw that all effort and all achievement come from men's envy of their fellow men." Therefore it is certainly not unthinkable that Ecclesiastes could be among the first of that exceptional line of theologians with insight enough to see that human greed and ambition can actually "be made to work for the common good." For instance, Ecclesiastes' assessment of human nature is very close to Pascal's, who can also tell us: "All men naturally hate one another. We employ our lusts as best we can in the service of the common good. But this is only a pretence and a false image of love, for at bottom it is nothing but hate" (Pascal, *The Pensées*, tr. J. M. Cohen [Baltimore: Penguin Books, 1961], p. 70).

21. Following the lead of the Swiss church's "Zurich Bible," I have transposed the preceding

verse's sentence about having "no burial" or "no funeral" to Ecclesiastes' description of the stillborn child. Translators of the Zurich Bible supposed this sentence to have been thus accidentally misplaced, a supposition which certainly makes clear sense of an otherwise difficult sentence. (See O. S. Rankin, in *The Interpreter's Bible*, p. 62).

22. More literally, "God made man upright, but they have sought out many devices" (RSV). Man's "upright" posture, among all the animals of creation, suggests his special relation to God. But instead men have willfully turned to "inventions" (so KJV) or "devices" of their own—i.e., to false gods.

23. For commentary on this verse see p. 108.

PART II

1. Heinz Zahrnt, *What Kind of God?* (Minneapolis: Augsburg Publishing House, 1971), pp. 151-52.

2. John Updike, *Rabbit Redux* (New York: Alfred A. Knopf, 1971), p. 125.

3. Robert Gordis, *Koheleth—The Man and His World* (New York: Schocken Books, 1968), p. 42.

4. Robert Gordis, *The Wisdom of Ecclesiastes* (New York: Behrman House, 1945), p. v.

5. Jürgen Moltmann, *Religion, Revelation and the Future* (New York: Charles Scribner's Sons, 1969), p. 43.

6. Gordis, *Koheleth—The Man and His World*, op. cit., p. vii.

7. Paul Tillich, *The New Being* (New York: Charles Scribner's Sons, 1955), p. 168.

8. Gaius Glenn Atkins, "The Book of Ecclesiastes—Exposition," *The Interpreter's Bible, Vol. V* (Nashville: Abingdon Press, 1956), p. 26.

9. Edgar Jones, *Proverbs and Ecclesiastes, Torch Bible Commentaries*, Vol. XVI (London: SCM Press, 1961), p. 275.

10. F. N. Jasper, "Ecclesiastes: A Note for Our Time," *Interpretation*, Vol. XXI, No. 3 (July 1967), p. 272.

11. Quoted in Heinz Zahrnt, *The Question of God* (New York: Harcourt, Brace and World, 1966), p. 145.

12. Karl Barth, *Church Dogmatics*, Vol. I/2 (Edinburgh: T. & T. Clark, 1956), p. 85.

13. H. Richard Niebuhr, *Radical Monotheism and Western Culture* (New York: Harper & Row, 1960), p. 52.

14. Zahrnt, *The Question of God, op. cit.*, p. 140.

15. Dietrich Bonhoeffer, *Letters and Papers from Prison*, rev. ed. (New York: The Macmillan Co., 1967), p. 200.

16. Karl Barth, *The Word of God and the Word of Man* (New York: Harper & Row, 1957), pp. 301, 309-10.

17. James W. Woelfel, *Bonhoeffer's Theology* (Nashville: Abingdon Press, 1970), pp. 232-33.

18. Walther Eichrodt, *Theology of the Old Testament*, Vol. II (Philadelphia: The Westminster Press, 1967), p. 161.

19. William Johnstone, "'The Preacher' As Scientist," *Scottish Journal of Theology*, Vol. 20 (1967), pp. 219, 218.

20. Gerhard von Rad, op. cit., p. 455.

21. Tillich, op. cit., p. 162.

22. Quoted in Zahrnt, *What Kind of God?, op. cit.*, p. 83.

23. Von Rad, *Old Testament Theology, op. cit.*, p. 456.

24. *Ibid.*, p. 453.

25. Eichrodt, op. cit., p. 161.

26. Zahrnt, *The Question of God, op. cit.*, p. 129.

27. T. S. Eliot, *The Complete Poems and Plays* (New York: Harcourt, Brace and Co., 1952), pp. 118, 209.

28. Gordis, *Koheleth—The Man and His World, op. cit.*, p. 384.

29. George A. Barton, *The Book of Ecclesiastes, International Critical Commentary* (New York: Charles Scribner's Sons, 1908), pp. 47, 50.

30. Von Rad, *Old Testament Theology, op. cit.*, p. 452.

31. Walter Harrelson, *Interpreting the Old Testament* (New York: Holt, Rinehart and Winston, Inc., 1964), p. 443.

32. Atkins, op. cit., pp. 22-23.

33. Johnstone, op. cit., p. 219.

34. Martin Luther, *Luther's Works*, Vol. 15 (St. Louis: Concordia Publishing, 1972), p. 9.

35. Barth, *The Word of God and the Word of Man, op. cit.*, p. 301.

36. William Ernest Henley, "Invictus," from *The Best Loved Poems of the American People* (Garden City: Garden City Publishing Co., 1936), p. 73.

37. Dietrich Bonhoeffer, *Ethics, op. cit.*, p. 19.

38. Martin Luther, *Works of Martin Luther,* Vol. VI (Philadelphia: Muhlenberg Press, 1932), p. 394.

39. Bernhard Anderson, *Understanding the Old Testament,* 2nd ed. (Englewood Cliffs: Prentice-Hall, 1966), p. 506.

40. R. B. Y. Scott, *The Way of Wisdom* (New York: The Macmillan Co., 1971), p. 180.

41. Walther Zimmerli, *op. cit.*, p. 158.

42. *Ibid.*, p. 156.

43. Quoted in Gabriel Vahanian, *The Death of God* (New York: George Braziller, 1961), p. x.

44. Johnstone, *op. cit.*, pp. 220-21.

45. Von Rad, *Old Testament Theology, op. cit.*, p. 456.

46. Bonhoeffer, *Letters and Papers from Prison, op. cit.*, p. 185.

47. Jones, *op. cit.*, p. 276.

48. Quoted in Arthur M. Schlesinger, Jr., *A Thousand Days* (Boston: Houghton Mifflin Co., 1965), p. 114.

49. Norman H. Snaith, "Grace," in *A Theological Word Book of the Bible,* ed. Alan Richardson (New York: The Macmillan Co., 1955), p. 102.

50. Gordis, *Koheleth—The Man and His World, op. cit.*, p. 40.

51. *Ibid.*

52. *The New American Bible* (New York: P. J. Kenedy & Sons, 1970), p. 898.

53. Jacques Ellul, *To Will and to Do* (Philadelphia: Pilgrim Press, 1969), p. 19.

54. Jones, *op. cit.*, p. 259.

55. *Koheleth—The Man and His World, op. cit.*, p. 74.

56. *The Jerusalem Bible* (Garden City: Doubleday and Co., 1966), p. 978.

57. *Koheleth—The Man and His World, op. cit.*, p. 17.

58. *The Jerusalem Bible, op. cit.*, p. 979.

59. The thesis that Ecclesiastes is himself the sole author of his book also finds well-founded support in the work of German theologian H. J. Blieffert. According to O. S. Rankin (*The Interpreter's Bible, op. cit.*, pp. 9-11), Blieffert holds that the question of Ecclesiastes' unity "can only be solved theologically. The contradictions within the book are explained by the quality of the mind of the author, which retained elements of traditional Judaism together with a lively secular outlook. . . . In Blieffert's view the correct conception of the quality of Ecclesiastes' thought renders unnecessary the theory of interpolations. . . . Koheleth, the man, is the unity in which the diversity of thought resides."

60. Atkins, *op. cit.*, p. 24.

61. Zimmerli, *op. cit.*, p. 157.

62. Von Rad, *Old Testament Theology, op. cit.*, p. 458.

63. Melville, *loc. cit.*

64. Bonhoeffer, *Letters and Papers from Prison, op. cit.*, p. 103.

PART III

1. Von Rad, "Typological Interpretation of the Old Testament," *Essays on Old Testament Hermeneutics,* ed. Claus Westermann (Richmond, Va.: John Knox Press, 1963), p. 39.

2. Quoted in Gordis, *Koheleth, op. cit.*, p. 5.

3. Jacques Ellul, *Hope in Time of Abandonment* (New York: The Seabury Press, 1973), p. 179.

4. Wilhelm Vischer, *The Witness of the Old Testament to Christ* (London: Lutterworth Press, 1949), pp. 7, 26, 30.

5. Von Rad, *Old Testament Theology,* Vol. II (New York: Harper & Row, 1965), p. 387.

6. Carl E. Braaten, *New Directions in Theology Today,* Vol. II, *History and Hermeneutics* (Philadelphia: The Westminster Press, 1966), p. 104.

7. Quoted by W. Baumgartner, "The Wisdom Literature," *The Old Testament and Modern Study,* ed. H. H. Rowley (Oxford: The Clarendon Press, 1952), p. 221.

8. *Ibid.*

9. Eichrodt, *op. cit.*, p. 161.

10. Zimmerli, *op. cit.*, p. 156.

11. Von Rad, *Old Testament Theology,* Vol. I, *op. cit.*, p. 454.

12. Anderson, *loc. cit.*

13. Braaten, *op. cit.*, p. 108.

14. Von Rad, *Old Testament Theology,* Vol. II, *op. cit.*, pp. 321, 319, 332, 361.

15. *Ibid.*, p. 381.

16. *Ibid.*, p. 363.

17. *Ibid.*, p. 414.

18. Johannes Hempel, "The Contents of the Lit-

erature of Israel," *Record and Revelation*, ed. H. Wheeler Robinson (Oxford: The Clarendon Press, 1938), p. 70.

19. Von Rad, *Old Testament Theology*, Vol. I, *op. cit.*, p. 455.

20. *Ibid.*, p. 453.

21. Vischer, *op. cit.*, p. 28.

22. *The Jerusalem Bible, op. cit.*, p. 979.

23. Von Rad, *Old Testament Theology*, Vol. II, *op. cit.*, pp. 422-23.

24. Karl Barth, *Church Dogmatics*, I/2, *op. cit.*, p. 349.

25. *Hamlet*, III, ii, 19.

26. Zahrnt, *What Kind of God? op. cit.*, p. 117.

27. Von Rad, *Old Testament Theology*, Vol. II, *op. cit.*, p. 368.

28. Von Rad, *Old Testament Theology*, Vol. I, *op. cit.*, p. 455.

29. Quoted in Zahrnt, *What Kind of God?, op. cit.*, p. 133.

30. Kornelis H. Miskotte, *When the Gods Are Silent* (London: Collins, 1967), p. 458.

31. Von Rad, *Old Testament Theology*, II, *op. cit.*, pp. 362-63, 415.

32. Zimmerli, "Promise and Fulfillment," *Essays on Old Testament Hermeneutics, op. cit.*, p. 120.

33. Barth, *Church Dogmatics*, I/2, *op. cit.*, p. 83.

34. Rankin, *op. cit.*, p. 19.

35. Tillich, *op. cit.*, pp. 162-63.

36. Zahrnt, *op. cit.*, p. 205.

37. Arthur C. Cochrane, "Joy to the World: The Message of Ecclesiastes," *The Christian Century*, Vol. LXXXV, No. 51 (December 18, 1968), p. 1598.

38. Eichrodt, *op. cit.*, p. 502.

39. Friedrich Nietzsche, *The Portable Nietzsche*, ed. Walter Kaufmann (New York: The Viking Press, 1954), pp. 434, 436.

40. Braaten, *op. cit.*, p. 97.

41. Anderson, *op. cit.*, p. 504.

42. Zahrnt, *What Kind of God?, op. cit.*, pp. 256-57.

43. Moltmann, *op. cit.*, p. 3.

44. Zimmerli, *Man and His Hope in the Old Testament* (Naperville, Ill.: Alec R. Allenson, Inc., 1968), p. 21.

45. Eichrodt, *op. cit.*, pp. 510-11.

46. Quoted in Barth, *Church Dogmatics*, II/2, *op. cit.*, p. 46.

47. Albert Camus, *The Myth of Sisyphus* (New York: Vintage Books, 1955), p. 91.

48. Camus, *The Fall* (New York: Alfred A. Knopf, 1958), pp. 115, 135.

49. Wilhelm Vischer, quoted in Gordis, *Koheleth—The Man and His World, op. cit.*, p. 5.

50. See Barton, *op. cit.*, p. 4.

51. Von Rad, *Old Testament Theology*, Vol. II, *op. cit.*, p. 363.

52. Zahrnt, *What Kind of God? op. cit.*, p. 51.

53. It is apparently this tradition that Karl Barth has in mind when he asks in *The Word of God and the Word of Man* (*op. cit.*, p. 62): "What is the key to the mind in which a book of such 'subdued enthusiasm' as Ecclesiastes could have been conceived? What is the secret of the man—call him a copyist who will!—who could baffle a historical dissecting expert by the genius he used in combining the two major sections of the two books of Isaiah into *one*?"

54. Zimmerli, "Promise and Fulfillment," *op. cit.*, p. 120.

55. Vischer, *op. cit.*, p. 33.

56. A. S. Peake, *The Problem of Suffering in the Old Testament* (London: Robert Bryant, 1904), p. 135.

57. Von Rad, *Old Testament Theology*, Vol. II, *op. cit.*, p. 337.

58. See Barton, *op. cit.*, pp. 4-5.

59. Barth, *Church Dogmatics*, III/4, *op. cit.*, p. 536.

60. Quoted in *The World Treasury of Religious Quotations*, ed. Ralph L. Woods (New York: Hawthorn Books, 1966), p. 65.

61. Gabriel Vahanian, *Wait without Idols* (New York: George Braziller, 1964), p. 245.

62. Zahrnt, *What Kind of God? op. cit.*, pp. 43, 45.

63. Atkins, *op. cit.*, p. 21.

64. A. F. Rainey, "A Study of Ecclesiastes," *Concordia Theological Monthly*, Vol. 35, No. 3 (March 1964), p. 148.

65. Albert Camus, *Resistance, Rebellion and Death* (New York: Alfred A. Knopf, 1961), pp. 70-71.